GET
EDUCATED!

THE MAN BEHIND
The Common Black College Application

Robert A. Mason, Jr.
Dr. Stacii Jae Johnson

Published by EDU, Inc.

ISBN: 978-0-578-39544-9

These are the members of my immediate family that my grandmother affectionately referred to as "The Mess." Included are my grandmother Edith Reid, my uncles Will Reid and Vic Reid, my aunt Constance Reid, and my mother Ernestine Mason. This book is dedicated to them and to my brother Todd Mason, who helped me to understand the meaning of family.

Table of Contents

Foreword

As a President of a Historically Black College and University (HBCU), I am intimately familiar with the economic challenges and hardships that many Black students throughout this country and abroad encounter when attempting to pursue their dreams of going to college. HBCUs have been the educational lifeline for our community since the late 1800s. Despite the seemingly insurmountable odds, each year students successfully matriculate at HBCUs nationwide and go on to excel in all areas of human endeavor including corporate America, government, law, medicine, education, sports, and the arts.

The Common Black College Application (CBCA) has played a pivotal role in the success of the more than 250,000 students who have completed the application. For twenty years, the CBCA has shifted the paradigm as to how students can apply to college, thereby increasing their educational opportunities. Equally as important, the CBCA has altered the landscape and eliminated many of the barriers that prevented many HBCUs from being able to recruit students both domestically and abroad.

The CBCA has been significant to college presidents around the country. It allows us to meet more students who seek to expand their career options and develop their potential. I encounter thousands of young Black students from various backgrounds who arrive on college campuses with passive, indifferent attitudes which are nurtured into competence, ambition, and a commitment to leave their mark on the world. HBCU graduates are commanded to be trailblazers—to go where there is no path and leave a trail.

This book chronicles the creation of the CBCA, and it is a clarion call to all those who dare to be great. Robert Mason personifies all that is the BLACK COLLEGE EXPERIENCE.

Dr. Glenda Baskin Glover
President of Tennessee State University
International President and Chief Executive Officer
Alpha Kappa Alpha Sorority, Inc. Term 2018 - 2022

Introduction

On May 30, 1960 at 3:46 p.m., I was born to Robert and Ernestine Mason at Burrell Memorial Hospital in Roanoke, VA. It was determined well in advance of my being born that I would be named after my father, Robert Allen Mason, Junior. Much to my father's chagrin, Junior was a moniker that I never fully adopted. Even some of my closest friends are not aware of the fact that I am a junior.

Me in 1961. I was the first-born son and the first grandson in the family.

As the first-born to my parents and the first grandson to both my paternal and maternal grandparents, I was constantly showered with love and affection. I was told my grandfather would often come to my parents' apartment before the break of day, demanding to see his grandson. Even if I was asleep, he would wake me up and insist that my mother dress me.

Immediately after I was dressed, he would whisk me away and not return for hours.

We lived in the Carver Apartments on a dead-end street in North West Roanoke. The apartments were directly across the street from where the city garbage trucks parked nightly. Periodically I am reminded of the pungent, putrid smell of garbage wafting through the air during sweltering summer days. From the time that I was born until I was six years old, I lived the carefree life of a child, concerned only about being with my friends, racing twigs in the curbside water after a rainfall, and playing cowboys and Indians on an enormous, tree-lined hill. This carefree life all came to a screeching halt when my parents divorced.

My mother and I, along with my younger brother who had been born a few years later, moved from Carver because she was unable to afford the rent. We moved to 1825 Liberty Road NW: the Lincoln Terrace Projects.

Lincoln Terrace was far different from Carver. It seemed the one- and two-floor red brick apartments extended as far as the eye could see.

One

Through the Eyes of a Child

Within a matter of weeks after we moved to Lincoln Terrace, we had to go to Big Mamma's funeral in Bluefield, West Virginia. Big Mamma was my mother's grandmother. When we came back, we walked into our apartment, and everything was gone. It just seemed so surreal. They even stole the carpets off the floor and the blankets off the beds.

I can remember being in a curious state. I didn't fully grasp what had happened. The most vivid memory I have is of my mom crying as she kept asking, "Why would somebody do this to us?" I think the one thing that affected me the most was that I lost my sense of security and that idyllic, childhood feeling that I had up until that very moment.

Over the next few days, I finally realized the gravity of what happened, and I was horrified. My brother and I slept in twin beds. I was so distraught and afraid from the break-in, I would put toys on the floor of my room because in the emotionally-jarred mind of an eight-year-old, if anybody walked into the room, they would step on one of the toys and I would hear them. Even to this day, when I stay in hotels, I don't stay on the ground floor. That lost sense of security I experienced as a child continues to haunt me as an adult.

There was another moment when the stark realities of the world were visited upon me as a child. I was about nine or ten at the time. I was in the closet playing, and I saw this Monopoly game. I opened the game and started playing with it. I was probably a little old to still be thinking there was a Santa, but my mom labored tirelessly to shield me and my brother from the hardships and realities that she suffered being a single parent raising two children alone in the Projects. Totally absorbed as I played with the Monopoly game, I suddenly realized that this was the very game that I had asked Santa to bring me for Christmas. At that moment, many of the fond memories I associated with Christmas faded away, replaced by the discovery of the cruel reality that there is no such thing as Santa Claus.

Although both events were traumatic, the break-in affected me far more profoundly. You may ask yourself, why would the discovery of there not being a Santa be so devasting? It's the loss of what Santa represented that was so life-altering. If Santa wasn't real, what else that I believed in so deeply as a child was imaginary? I am not a mental health professional, but I would assume that when one's reality as a child has been shattered, he or she begins to question what else is not real—a state that can foster feelings of fear and anxiety, and thoughts of being alone in the world.

The break-in, on the other hand, has been far more debilitating, and has had a deleterious effect on my psyche. To this day, I am consumed with a concern for safety and security. I am always keenly aware of my surroundings; so much so that it borders on paranoia.

TEASING

More than any other experience of my childhood, the fact that I was teased as a child has shaped my character and contributed to the adult that I have become. The humiliation I endured impacted me so much that as an adult, I am often brought to tears when I see others express feelings of sadness, embarrassment, or self-doubt.

The source of the teasing was a green stain that was on my top front teeth. Other kids used to call me "Mr. Green Jeans" after a character on the kid's program, *Captain Kangaroo*. I don't have a clue how it happened, but as I got older, the green stain went away.

The teasing was difficult for me, but I was often also shunned by some of the neighborhood kids. Stephen and his sister lived across the yard directly behind our apartment. They would always play together with Teresa, who lived next door to them. Occasionally, I would play with them, but on one particular day we were playing together, and it started to rain. Stephen said to everyone, "Come on, let's go in my house." We all started to run towards Stephen's house, and he held out his hand pointing at me and said, "No, not you Rob." I couldn't understand why I was not allowed to go with everyone else into Stephen's house, but there was nothing I could do but go home. I was devastated as I walked into my house and up to my room, from where I could see them running in and out of Stephen's house laughing and having fun. I'm getting emotional as I am typing this. I guess the pain of that moment has never gone away.

The teasing and the occasional bullying eventually stopped when James and I started playing on the same little league football team. James was one of the two kids on my block that teased and bullied me. We eventually became really good friends. James died of leukemia at ten years old. I had no concept of death. I just kept wondering why James wasn't coming out to play anymore.

As an adult, I am less inclined to be intimidated. More importantly, the bullying and teasing I experienced has given way to a heightened sense of empathy for others. I am a far better person today because of the ridicule, the teasing, and the pain I experienced as a child.

5

TWO

Family Matters

MOM, MY EVERYTHING

My mother recently said to me, "I wish I had given you something to be proud of." I watched my mom struggle to raise two black males in a housing project, alone. There are few people that I respect more than her. She worked tirelessly to do all that she could to ensure that my brother and I wanted for nothing. She never bought one of us something without buying the other something of comparable value. If my mom bought me a new pair of shoes, she bought my brother a new pair of shoes.

My mom worked in retail all her life. Up until I went to college, she worked in the men's department at the Heironimus Department Store in downtown Roanoke. Retail did a lot for my mom. Despite not going to college, she still got what I would consider to be an informal education working at Heironimus. In order to interface with the public, one has to have a skillset and the ability to communicate.

My mom was accepted into high school; however, she was not able to attend because she had to work to help take care of her siblings.

Mom didn't make much money, but she did the absolute best she could for my brother and me. There was never much food in the refrigerator. My friends, mostly Eric, would come over and go in the refrigerator looking for something to eat. Often, before I could stop him, he would open the door and laughingly say, "You don't have any food in here." Trying to hide my embarrassment,

I'd say, "My mom hasn't gone to the grocery store yet." Countless times, my brother and I would ask my mom what we were going to eat for dinner, and she would say, "There may not be anything in the kitchen that you want to eat, but there's food in there."

My mother and I only saw each other occasionally during the week because of her work schedule and my being in school and involved in sports. Much of my time was spent with coaches and my friends. Practically all of my friends were being raised by their mothers. Our coaches looked out for us and were like surrogate fathers. They would come pick us up and bring us halfway across the city to go to practice and then bring us back to the Projects.

My dad, through no real fault of his own, wasn't in my life to any great extent. If you asked me how much time I spent with my dad from age three to age fifteen, I would answer, "Hours." Coaches were the first male figures to play a pivotal role in my life.

My mother and father on their wedding day in 1959.

DIVORCE DECREE

My mother and father divorced when I was six years old. My dad was in the Air Force, and after the divorce, he moved to Maryland and remained there until he died. He remarried twice.

7

I can remember sitting on the couch in between my mother and father when I was about seven or eight and my father asking who I wanted to live with. I chose to live with my mom.

Although he lived in Maryland, he would come home occasionally because my grandmother still lived in Roanoke. When he was there, he would come and see my brother and me. My father was a great provider, and he absolutely loved my mom. Because of the divorce, it seemed my father's role in my life was defined by the checks I would anxiously await to receive on my birthdays and Christmas.

My father and me in 2000.

I think that I learned how to express love in the same way—by ensuring that those I love are always cared for through a check, rather than being there for them in far more significant ways—emotionally and spiritually. For much of his life, my father was an alcoholic. This is a trait I definitely inherited from him. At one point he tried to get custody of my brother and me, but it didn't work out. Although I know my dad loved both of us with all his heart, one of my biggest regrets is that he never saw me play one basketball or football game. Every summer we would go visit him in Maryland. I remember that once he promised we were going to the beach to go crabbing. I got up early the next morning excited and ready to go, but my dad ended up spending the entire day doing what he did almost the entire time we were in Maryland visiting him: sitting in his favorite chair, drinking. I remember that being one of the most disappointing times I had ever spent with him during our trips to Maryland.

There was never a time when I didn't have a lot of toys. My mom, trying to be a good parent, attempted to replace my dad by buying us toys. I remember having a yard sale as a child and selling my toys to make money. I don't know where that entrepreneurial spirit came from, but this and countless similar instances like that have occurred throughout my life, and have undoubtedly led to the creation of the Common Black College Application (CBCA).

TODD

There is a five-year age difference between my brother Todd and me. I was far from a loving and caring big brother to Todd until I was in my late teens. It's one the biggest regrets of my life. If I had the opportunity to do one thing over in my life, it would be to have treated Todd far better when we were young.

My brother Todd at age seven.

9

In 1992, Todd moved to Atlanta. The first year he stayed with me. I have tried in my adult life to be a much better brother. As I indicated earlier, much to my chagrin, I often show my love by writing a check—a behavior that I realize is far from exemplary. Although the age difference when we were young and my intense focus on the CBCA more recently has sometimes complicated our relationship, we love each other dearly.

I HAD PRAYING GRANDMOTHERS

My father mother's name was Doretha Board. We called her She-She. She was extremely stern. My mother's grandmother was named Edith Reid. We called her Mammaw. Neither of them had more than a sixth-grade education. They were both devoted, churchgoing women. However, She-She cursed like a sailor, smoked, and was a stern, spare-the-rod-and-spoil-the-child kind of grandmother. Mammaw never cursed. She never wore pants. She was a maid for a wealthy White family for a substantial part of her adult life, and she never met a person she didn't like. To grow up with that dichotomy is significant to who I am today.

Since I was the oldest grandson, when she gave Christmas presents, Mammaw would always give me money. She would always sneak me a little extra money and say, "I know you're a little older, so here's a little extra change." As we got into our late teens, we didn't see She-She much unless my father was in town.

I never wanted to go to either of my grandmothers' houses, but the one thing I absolutely loved about both of them was their cooking. It always amazed me how both of them could make biscuits that tasted so dramatically different and both be so amazingly good. I spent more time with Mammaw because of my mom. If my mom needed something, Mammaw would catch a bus, and we would meet her at the bus stop. Rather than her getting off the bus and having to pay another bus fare, she would just give us money or a bag of groceries and then ride the bus back home.

WILL I AM

Will, Gayle, and Vick were my mother's siblings. Will was my everything. He was my protector. Will is who I am. I look like Will. I wanted to talk like Will, I wanted to drive like Will, I wanted to walk like Will. Everything that Will did, I wanted to do. He was "that guy" to me. He was cool even when he drove. He was always immaculately dressed unless he was working, and his shoes were ALWAYS spit-shined. That is another trait I emulated.

He was a good-looking guy—definitely a ladies' man. He was about 5′8″ and had a robust, distinct laugh, and no matter where you were in the house, you would hear him. He had a medium complexion with "good" hair, as they say. He loved his nephew (me) to death. Will never missed a game in which I played. Will loved kids, and he married a woman who had six children.

Will was the maintenance man in Lincoln Terrace, the Projects in which I grew up. I remember once I was visiting a girl's house in the Project at about two in the morning. I heard someone coming through the back door. I looked up, and it was Will coming through the door. He was seeing the mom of the girl whose house I was visiting. We looked at each other and just smiled as he went upstairs.

Will was there for me no matter what, through the drugs, the alcohol—anything that I needed, he was always there. Will passed away at a fairly young age, in his mid-sixties. He was a chain smoker and died of cancer.

Gayle is my mom's sister. She helped to foster a sense of adventure in me. She passed away a few years ago. I have never thought of myself as smart. I think I process information well, but Gayle was one of the smartest people in our family. She didn't go to college, but she was one of those people that was well-read and very articulate. Gayle was a voracious reader. She played a vital role in our family because she was fearless. Gayle was strong-willed and never backed down from anything.

11

Once, when I was eleven, Todd and I were visiting Gayle in New York, which is where she lived at the time. My brother and I were pretty much left at home when Gayle went to work, and one day, I just decided to go out into the city on my own. It was a different New York then, and you didn't have to fear for kids like you do now.

I believe that my unyielding curiosity and sense of adventure has led to my fearless nature when it comes to exploring new places and things. I always felt even as a child that there was more out there than the Lincoln Terrace Projects.

My Uncle Vick left Roanoke to go into the military when he was in his early twenties. It was always a special time when Vick came home. He would stay at Mammaw's house. The whole family would come over and Mammaw would cook. I can remember sitting on the floor in the entrance to the kitchen listening to them tell stories about the past. It always amazed me that Mammaw had this large living room but the entire family would always end up crowded in the kitchen, sharing their memories often late into the early morning hours. It seems almost instinctive that family would gather in this tiny kitchen to share what can be best described as an oral history.

I wasn't as close to my family on my father's side. Many of them moved to D.C. when I was young.

Three

Best Friends for Life

ERIC JOHNSON

Eric has been my best friend for over fifty years, although we're complete opposites. We met around the fifth grade. There were six or seven of us in the group, many of whom are in this picture. Eric and I gravitated towards each other. He's the type of friend that, if I had a sister, I would approve of them getting married.

Robert Mason and Eric Johnson at the Youth Football Banquet in 1972.

At that time, one of the pivotal moments in Eric's life was fighting Ricky Wright. Ricky was also one of our best friends. Fighting Ricky was a breakthrough for Eric. Our Projects were not nearly as bad as Projects are now, but there was a hierarchy.

Ricky wasn't a bully, but he was good with his hands, so he stood at the top of the fisticuff food chain, so to speak.

On this particular day Eric and Ricky had an altercation, and Eric stood up to him and fought Ricky. I am not one to say who won the fight, but that day changed Eric's life. It definitely bolstered Eric's rep in the Project.

By the time we were in ninth grade, Eric and I were beginning to be known around Roanoke as the cool kids. I was known as a good athlete, a decent-looking kid, and a "showoff." I wanted to be the coolest kid in the Projects, and I made a concerted effort to be. As a teenager, a premium is placed on dancing and being able to dress. I could do both well. We would go to parties and people would say as we were coming through the door, "That's Rob and Eric."

One night, Eric and I went to a party miles away from where we lived. I'm not sure how we got there, but someone had to have given us a ride because it was too far from our house to walk. We were in the ninth grade. The party was for a guy named Jake. Jake lived in upper northwest where many of the professionals, schoolteachers and preachers lived—on the other side of tracks. Jake was probably twenty years old. He let us in his party because we were the cool kids, and he said, "Go dance with the girls." We were having a great time, and then an epiphany occurred: "How the hell are we going to get home?" It was too far to walk, and it was two o'clock in the morning.

Walter Brown gave us a ride to the dump, the city landfill, which was right across the street from the Projects. The dump was pitch black. As soon as we got out of the car, Eric and I walked for about three yards, and we both started running towards our houses as fast as we could. It was so dark that you could barely see your hand in front of your face.

I tried to sneak into the house. As I was walking into my room my mom asked, "Where have you been? It's two o'clock in the morning." I said, "I was out with Eric," as if that was going to make everything all right. Without raising her voice, she said, "Don't you go out of this house tomorrow." That was normally our punishment for misbehaving. My mother rarely would "beat" us. Instead, we were not allowed to go out of the house the next day. That was the life that we led. That's what it was like being raised in the Projects by a single parent who was trying to figure out how to cope with and raise two black sons.

SHOW ME THE WAY

Darnell Wood is the reason that I went to Virginia State University. He was two years ahead of me in school. The Woods lived a few blocks away from the Projects. There were five boys and two girls. All their names started with the letter D. Darnell and I played football together in high school. When he was a senior, I was a sophomore. We played in the same defensive backfield at Patrick Henry High School.

He was the first person I knew to attend college. He came back home that summer, and you could tell that he had changed. During one conversation with him, he suggested we should go to homecoming in the fall.

My brother, Eric, and I ended up going to Virginia State for homecoming later in the year. We had a great time, but I was hurling in the car all the way back to Roanoke. I drank both beer and cheap wine by the glass full the night before. As a result, I had a massive hangover. Not a great example for your younger brother.

By then, I was drinking a fair amount. In ninth grade, I once decided to buy two quarts of Schlitz Malt Liquor Bull rather than going to school. I left home as if I was going to school and instead, I went to Neighbors Store and waited outside for someone that I could persuade to buy the beer for me. I had to be careful because I knew mom would be riding a bus that went right by the store. Every time a bus would come, I would hide behind the store.

Finally, I saw one my friend's older brothers named Ralph. I asked him to buy the beer for me, and he agreed. I gave him the $2.25. While I was giving Ralph the money, another bus came by, and I almost forgot to hide. He laughed, took my money, and went into the store to buy the beer. He came out, gave me the two quarts of beer in a brown paper bag, and said laughing, "You still hiding from buses?" I took the beer and responded in my tough guy voice, "I'm not hiding from nothing." I walked across the dump toward school. I went down near the school track where there was a big rock to sit on and drink the beer. There was something about opening that beer, smelling that aroma and feeling the warm sun beaming on my face—life just didn't get any better than this.

After drinking the beer, I was feeling a bit buzzed. I clearly could not go to school, so I decided to go back home. My mom went to work at nine o'clock and didn't come home until five. I laid down until it was time to go to football practice.

I didn't realize I had a problem with alcohol until after college. I didn't even like beer when I first started drinking it. I didn't start to like beer until I got to college. In high school, I drank because I wanted to get drunk; but in college, I actually started to like the taste.

ADDISON MIDDLE SCHOOL FOOTBALL

I played Little League Football from age eight to age fourteen. By eighth grade, I had started to truly blossom as an athlete, and in the ninth grade I played for Addison Middle School.

That particular year, Addison brought together some of the best athletes in the city. Both the male and female teams won every sport. Four of us were picked to be in *The Roanoke Times*, which was the city newspaper.

I played receiver. I scored on every team in the league, all six middle schools. I even scored a touchdown in the championship game, but I wasn't picked for the All-Star team. That's something that disturbs me even today.

In ninth grade, we had a student tradition called "Ninth Grade Day." It was a day that ninth graders skipped school. I was walking to school and when I got there, the guys said, "After first period, we're going over to Michael Olsen's house." I said, "For what?" They said, "We're going to get high." So we all gave five dollars to the cause.

I wasn't really a weed smoker, but I didn't want to be left out. Ricky was one of the best basketball players in the city, even in the ninth grade. He had been smoking weed for as long as I had been drinking, and he was coordinating this effort. We all gave our money to him. Besides, getting the weed was all his idea. About ten of us chipped in on the weed and left school after first period. Ricky bought the weed, and we all went over to Michael's house and got high. We were just passing one joint after another. Next thing I know, I was so damn high I felt like the couch was absorbing me. I started to realize that I needed to get out of there, so I stumbled out of Michael's house and started to walk home.

That particular day, my mom was off from work. As I walked in the door, she was vacuuming. She turned off the vacuum and asked, "Why are you home so early? Is there something wrong?" I said, "Nothing is wrong. I just need to lay down." For all intents and purposes, I was a good kid. You have to understand, by this time, in her mind, I was well on my way to becoming a man. Mom never did drugs. She barely drank anything other than a glass of wine. Mom probably wouldn't know what it was if she smelled the weed on me. I just went to my room and laid down. When I got up, there was no issue.

HOME & GARDEN

Although we lived in the Projects, our house looked as if it could have been featured in an issue of *Home and Garden* magazine. Our bathroom was better decorated than most people's living rooms. As a matter of fact, I know my mom would have been a phenomenal interior decorator if given the opportunity. You never felt like you were in the Projects when you walked in our apartment. No matter how harsh the reality was just outside our doors, when I walked in to our apartment, the challenges I may have been facing at that time didn't seem so dire.

Growing up in the Projects, I found that I often overcompensated when interacting with people. I wanted to demonstrate that I was just as good as anyone else. For much of my life, in fact, I have felt that I was intellectually inferior. Even now, as an adult, I still have an inferiority complex; it just manifests itself in different ways.

It's only been within the last ten years that I've gotten to a place where I'm comfortable with who I am. A lot of that can be directly attributed to this "level of success" that I've been able to achieve with the CBCA. I'm not sure that I would be as grounded as I am, if I had not been able to achieve what I've accomplished thus far in life, almost solely as a result of the CBCA.

I was an extremely scholarly elementary school student and earned very good grades. But when I entered middle school my grades dropped precipitously. My only saving grace was that my mom always kept books in the house and in a state of extreme boredom, I would invariably read them. From the time I was in the first grade, I read above grade level. I never thought of myself as "smart" and still don't, but I can process information well, and I've become fairly articulate over the years. That allows me to mask my intellectual insecurities.

Mr. James, my middle school history teacher, used to make us do current event reports, and that was the last time I actually remember anybody questioning me about homework or schoolwork. My mom was trying to feed and clothe me. She didn't have time to be overly concerned about my grades. I truly did not take a book home from the time that I was in seventh grade to the time I graduated from high school. Of course, I may have done some work in class, but I honestly don't remember. As I sit here writing this book, I don't have any recollection of doing any homework or even taking a book home. Back then, you were not required to have certain grades to stay on the team in middle or high school. As a result, I was able to participate in any sport without fear of being put off the team because of my grades.

Four
A Different Path

I remember one time, some friends came by my house and said, "Come on, Rob. We're going to walk to Eureka Park for the game." After hearing my friends calling me, my mother came into my room and said, "You are not walking to Eureka Park." I am not sure why she reacted the way she did other than to say maybe she felt it was too far, although it was only about a thirty-minute walk. I pleaded with her to let me walk with the guys, telling her, "Everybody is walking except me." She emphatically said, "No. Those other boys are not my children." She decided that if I wanted to go, she would put me in a taxi. I mention this story because it was not an isolated incident. It is an example of how I was treated by my family.

Another time, when I was shooting craps on the corner by the bus stop with some older boys from the Projects, my mother got off the bus and saw me kneeling, getting ready to throw the dice. She grabbed me by the back of my shirt and practically dragged me down the street to our apartment. The entire time she kept repeating, "I did not raise you to be out here on the corner like some hoodlum, shooting dice."

I always viewed myself as different. I don't know if it was because of the way my family treated me as the oldest son and grandson, or how society treated me because of my athletic success. That's why when I look at where I am and what I've been able to accomplish, I don't know if I'm surprised because I always felt that there was something different in store for me. That may sound a bit conceited, but that's how it was.

There were two high schools in my hometown. William Fleming was probably 60% to 70% black. Patrick Henry, my high school, was probably 30% black, if that. Most of the affluent blacks—the sons and daughters of teachers and preachers—went to Fleming. At PH, most of the blacks came from Lincoln Terrace Projects, Southwest Projects, and other less affluent areas. There was no junior varsity football team at Patrick Henry. Everybody played on the varsity. You either made the team, or you didn't.

PATRICK HENRY HIGH SCHOOL

Coach Merrill Rosen was the head coach. He was no more than 5'5", but he commanded respect. He had won two state championships, one in West Virginia and one at Patrick Henry. He smoked a pipe and carried a clipboard seemingly at all times. He had a gruff, high-pitched voice that one could hear all the way across the field. I remember telling a friend I was going to try out for the team. He said that I would never make it, and if I made the team that I definitely wouldn't start. He was going into his junior year, and I would be a sophomore. He was on the team, and I guess because he didn't start, he assumed that I would not start either.

It was time for Captain's Practice to start. During Captain's Practice, we only wore shorts and a helmet, no pads, and we only went through some light drills. But the day of reckoning was approaching. After about a week, we put the pads on and started to hit each other. It was a little frightening, but I started to shine. It was time for Defensive Back Coach Wales to pick the starting defensive players. When he got to the defensive backs, he said, "Mason, I want you to play the left defensive back position." They put Frank Dent, who was also a sophomore, in the right defensive back position. This was practically unheard of, to have two sophomores in starting positions on the defense. I immediately looked at my friend who said I wouldn't make the team. Not only did I make the team, but I was starting as a sophomore.

We went to scrimmage a school called Northside. Everything was going well until halfway through the scrimmage. A receiver came out, I broke down into my stance, and he got by me and caught a touchdown. Coach Rosen was livid, "Mason, get your f---king ass off the field!"

From that point on, I didn't start the first four games. I only played on the kickoff team. That was a real blow to my ego. I had never not started in any sport that I'd ever played in my life. Looking back, that taught me about being disciplined enough to do what you're taught to do in different situations and not comprise or make allowances when faced with adversity. I didn't do what I was supposed to do. My assignment was to guard this one receiver and not be concerned about anything else that was going on around me, but I didn't do that. I strayed and broke the scheme. I was looking at the backfield to the quarterback and trying to read him, as opposed to looking at the player that I should have been defending.

There are a lot of parallels in life to what I was feeling during this period. There have been many times where I've suffered what many may perceive to be borderline failure, which is where I was at that point. It was the worst I'd ever felt. To think that I wasn't starting was devastating.

But no matter what happens or how devastating it is, I can process the circumstances in a way that allows me to move on. I can continue. I learned at a very early age—as a result of these kinds of challenges happening in my life—that you can do two things when something happens to you. You can change the condition, or you can change the way you think about the condition.

In this particular case, as a result of not doing what I was instructed to do, I suffered the consequence and was not able to begin the season at the starting defensive back position. Four games into the season, the person that took my position got beat by a receiver at practice, and Coach said, "Mason, get in there." I was back on the starting team. It was the Monday before the Shrine Bowl, the biggest game in the city.

SHRINE BOWL

We were playing our crosstown rival, William Fleming High School. All I could think about was that I was back on the starting team, and I was not going to blow this opportunity. All that week, I kept thinking, "I am back!" Even more, I was making my comeback just before the biggest game of the season and the biggest game I had ever played in my life up to that point. My coach said, "It's not what you eat the night before, it's what you eat forty-eight hours before that will impact your performance." I made sure I ate right. I got plenty of sleep. I didn't eat the junk that I would normally eat. With each day, my excitement grew that much more because everyone was talking about the game, including the city paper, The Roanoke Times.

We had a game-day routine that no one on the team would go home after school. We would stay and eat a meal before the game, watch films in the field house, and then get dressed and go to the stadium. The offense and defense did a walk-through of what they were going to be doing. I played both offense and defense, which is another thing that was rare for a sophomore.

When we got to the game, and they called my name, and I ran out on the field, it was like, "This is real. This is what it's all about." The players who had already been introduced were standing in two lines on the field, and I ran down the middle. My mom, my uncle, and my brother were all there. They never missed a game.

The game started, and we were going back and forth. Fleming scored first, and then we scored. It was seven to seven. Then they put me in on offense, and my play was called. Mike, the quarterback, looks at me and says, "I'm coming to you." I go out five yards, do a cut, and I catch the pass. This is huge. This is a sophomore on a varsity team. My childhood friend, Cheatwood, was a sophomore starting for Fleming. We're close, so we're talking on the field. "I'll see you at McDonald's after the game, but I'm going to kill you in a minute," said Cheatwood.

It was the early fourth quarter and the game was still tied seven to seven. I was playing defensive back, and I saw the Fleming quarterback drop back. I was on my guy and all of a sudden, I saw the ball coming my way. I broke on the ball and intercepted it and almost scored. Again, I was a sophomore in the biggest game of the year, and I had just intercepted the ball with the game tied. We went on to score and win the game.

I was elated. I was on cloud nine. I was running around after the game, and I thought I heard someone say, "Robert Mason." but I didn't pay attention to it. The guys were calling me: "Rob! Rob! Rob! They're calling you! The announcer is calling you to the field where the trophies are being given away. You won best defensive back!" I said, "What? What does that mean?" They said, "Go over there and get the trophy!"

I got the trophy, and I didn't know what to do. I ran it over to my mom and gave it to my uncle Will. Everybody was excited. Will was running around screaming, "That's my nephew! That's my nephew!" I won Best Defensive Back in the Shrine Bowl. That was the first time a sophomore had won that award in the Shrine Bowl, a legendary game that has been played for years.

After the game, we were riding home on the activity bus, and everybody was extremely excited. The activity bus took students home that were involved in different sports or activities who didn't have any other means of transportation after school hours. Coach Casey drove us home on the activity bus after the game. Coach was like a father to many of the black players on the team. As I was getting off the bus at my stop, Coach said, "That was a hell of a game you played, Mason."

I thanked him and ran in the house and asked mom if she had a couple of dollars. By now, she was home from the game. She gave me the money, and I ran out to meet George, who was the running back on the team. He had a car. Daryl, Darnell's brother, and George would always come to pick me up after the home games. We would always go to George's house before we went to McDonald's after the game. I'm not sure why, but I didn't complain because I wanted to go to McDonald's and then to the party.

George's father was an attorney. While we were there, Mr. Harris said, "Is that Mason?" I said, "Yes, sir." Then he said, "Good game, son." I tried to not show how excited I was to hear Mr. Harris comment on my game. I had no idea Mr. Harris knew who I was.

Everybody went to McDonald's after the game from both Fleming and PH. This night, it was packed. You couldn't tell me anything. I was walking on air. After we ate, George, Darrell, and I went to the party. One guy that I ended up going to Virginia State with, a guy named Chuck who played for Fleming, walked up to me at the party later that night and said, "You didn't deserve that trophy." I said, "Bro, were you even on the field? Who the hell are you?"

That was even more gratifying. That's where I was at that point in my life. I was this arrogant, egotistical kid, and that trophy didn't help. To think that a few weeks before, I had been in the depths of depression because I wasn't playing. I went from as low as I could possibly be to as high as I could possibly go. By that point, I had proved my worth by winning that trophy, and I no longer thought about not making the All-Star team the year before in middle school.

That year, we went seven and two, which is not bad. We played two teams that beat the brakes off of us, E.C. Glass and G.W. Danville. The Shrine Bowl was the pivotal moment. It catapulted me to a place where I was now recognized as one of the best players on the team, a reputation that lasted the next two years. Now everybody knew who I was.

Because I went to PH, I was developing a dual life. I would hang out in Southwest, which was where the White people lived. I would go to keg parties with the White girls and my boys that played on the football team until 11:00 p.m. Then I'd go over to my side of town and hang out until 2:00 a.m.

Football season was over, and basketball season was starting. I was a good basketball player, although not as good as I was in football. Unlike football, PH had a JV basketball team. Coach Thomas was the basketball coach, and he absolutely loved me. Again, I was a good kid and well respected throughout the school. Coach's wife was great. She would bake us chocolate chip cookies that were beyond delicious. Coach would always sneak me extra cookies. I was the high scorer on the JV team. There was always something about running out onto the basketball court in high school that was more exciting than in football because the crowd was so close to you. When you are introduced before a football game, it doesn't have the same level of intimacy as being introduced before a basketball game.

I remember once, after a game with Franklin County, Glen the scorekeeper came running into the locker room and shouted, "Rob, you had 39 points!" Coach Thomas sternly chastised Glen, "Glen, we don't do that here. We don't tell people how many they scored." The coach didn't want him stressing what one individual player had done because it was a team sport. But I was a ball hog. I wanted to score. I wanted to score every touchdown, every goal. I was just like most other star athletes who want the ball all the time.

We had Hall Principals and School Principals. Mr. Akin was my Hall Principal. He kept me out of a lot of trouble in high school. He always wanted what was best for me. He put me in the field house in middle school during a riot when I was at Addison Middle School. He always tried to make sure that I was taking the right classes. I wasn't doing all that well in the classes, but I was still taking college prep courses.

In my junior year, the newspaper was on campus taking pictures of the team and certain players. I was one of those players. The sports editor's name was John Whitfield, and he had a daughter named Cynthia that attended PH. She was also a cheerleader. She absolutely loved me to death. Some would say I was in the paper more than I should have been because of her father.

One Sunday, there was an article about me in the paper with a large picture of me dribbling a basketball. It would not have been uncommon for me to be in the paper for football, but basketball? I must admit, I was surprised when my mom came in my room and said, "There is someone from the newspaper on the phone for you." It was Mr. Whitfield. We talked for about thirty minutes. There is actually a copy of the article in my Hall of Fame Case at PH.

We didn't eat breakfast in the mornings before school because my mom had to go to work. I would normally buy one or two donuts after first period. Dutch crumble was my favorite. There were two classes I never missed. Coach White, my Defensive Coordinator, taught math, and Mr. Ponder taught biology. Mr. Ponder was the coolest teacher in the school. He had a big Afro, and he was a great tennis player. He played jazz during class. I honestly can't think of one class that I did well in, but I did like Mr. Ponder's class because he would play jazz music.

I had a good football year my junior year and ended up making All-Metro, which is an All-Star team. Making the All-Star team as a high school junior gave me a sense of validation. When basketball season started, I was on the varsity team. I didn't start, though, and that was devastating. I had started in every sport that I'd ever played, all my life. I was sitting on the bench now every game or only getting in with a few minutes left. That was one of the most difficult periods in my life, especially after coming off a banner year of football.

Basketball season always started even before football season had ended. As a result, I went almost literally from the football field to the basketball court. Although I am far better in football, I've always considered myself an above-average basketball player. The guy that was starting in front of me was older, and although I am reluctant to admit it, he was better. It didn't bother me that someone who was starting in front of me was better. What bothered me most was that I was benched for the first time in my life. That's all I cared about. It got so bad that one time after I didn't play, I came home crying uncontrollably. I went into the closet because I didn't want to wake my mom. She came in and said, "Rob, what's wrong?" I said, "Mom, I didn't play."

I don't know if that moment was more difficult for me or for her. I know it was hard for her to see her son in that state. I never wanted to worry my mom. Even to this day, if something happens, if there is something wrong, I won't tell her.

Getting through my junior year was tough. I never started the whole year. Not once. I had just come off the JV basketball team where I was the leading scorer. Now, I was sitting on the bench. I played, but I never started that whole year.

One thing that is a big deal about football is the letter jacket. I got a varsity letter in track my sophomore year and a varsity letter in football. My junior year, I got the letter in basketball too. That's when I lettered in all three sports. When my football letter jacket finally came with that number 45 on it, I was elated. I selected 45 because of Nicholas Sims. Nicholas came up in the Projects and was a player that I respected greatly. He went to Hampton University.

I didn't have girlfriends back then. Even to this day, I have never had many girlfriends. I see a lot of women though, and in high school, it was pretty much the same thing. I had dates for both my junior and senior proms, but I wasn't the type that you would see with a girlfriend at McDonald's, the mall, the movies, or at a party until I saw Denise Anderson at McDonald's after one of our games. She went to Fleming. She was one of those girls that was fairly quiet and didn't go out to parties much. She was drop-dead gorgeous. I would see her a few more times at McDonald's, but I was always afraid to introduce myself, so I did what I normally do. I would see a girl out somewhere that I liked, and then I would find someone I knew that knew her number. I started asking around and got Denise's number. I probably called and hung up two or three times. I would practice. I would put on some Barry White and create a little mood to hype myself up. When I finally called her, I said the same old thing: "Hey, Denise. You don't know who this is. My name is Rob. I'm number 45 for PH." It worked. We started talking, and before I knew it, we had been on the phone for two hours.

Denise was the first female I knew that had two parents in the home. I had never met somebody's father before. I wanted to take Denise to the prom. I finally got up enough courage to ask her, and she said yes. I borrowed my Uncle Will's car. When I picked Denise up, the car broke down outside of her house. It got overheated.

We finally got to the prom, and afterwards we went out to eat. After that, we were boyfriend/girlfriend, and we talked every day. The good thing about Denise was that she would go home about 9:00 p.m. Wherever we were, she was in by nine, so I was free to go out and party with my friends after that.

HIGH SCHOOL SENIOR YEAR

When I got to my senior year, I asked my mom if we could get a car. My mom had good credit, and my dad agreed to help pay for the car. I was in twelfth grade, living in the Projects, and I had a car. Everybody else was riding the bus to school. I was already thinking, I was the man, and now I had a car. It was a gold Volkswagen Wagon with no heat, no air conditioning, and a radio that you could barely hear. Everybody knew my car. It was always full of beer cans. Every Sunday after a game, I'd have to take my mom to church, and she would say, "We have to get the beer cans out," because we had to pick up my grandmother.

In high school, we were drinking two or three cases every Friday and Saturday. We would buy a six-pack to start, and I would drink four before Eric had a chance to drink two. Then we'd go get another six-pack. We would drink whatever our money could buy.

One day, I was on the way to class with Ricky and Chris, a tall White guy who played center on the basketball team. Ricky said, "Come on, Rob. We're going to get high." Chris had an old Mercedes. We went out to his car and rode around the corner and smoked two joints. We decided to go back to school, which was a bad idea.

I was late getting to Spanish class, and I ended up sitting in the back. Everything was a blur at this point, and the teacher asked me, "Mr. Mason, come up and read this passage." I got up, and I was scared as hell because I knew I was high. I believed that everyone else knew I was high, too.

I fumbled through reading the passage. She said, "Okay, read the next passage." I messed around and read the same passage that I had read already because I was just so damn high. She suspiciously asked, "Mr. Mason, are you okay?" I said, "Yeah, I'm good. Why? What's wrong?" She said, "You just read the exact same passage." Everybody just broke out in laughter. I said, "I need to leave."

I ended up leaving, and I think she told my basketball coach because that day before practice, he gave this talk about the importance of not using drugs, looking directly at me. Ricky and Jeff used to get high before practically every game. I think Coach had to know. But Coach saw me in a different light. I was perceived as a good kid. One of the statements that Coach made when I was inducted into the Hall of Fame was that everybody

I was inducted into the Patrick Henry Hall of Fame with Reginald Hayes in 1994.

knew me and liked me. I was a team leader and a good kid. Bear in mind, when Coach made that comment, he was supposed to be introducing my childhood friend Reggie, who was being inducted into the Hall of Fame at the same time. Coach ended up talking more about me than Reggie for the first few minutes, but he eventually talked about what a great track athlete Reggie was and how much he admired him.

By then, mom had taken on a second job cleaning a beauty salon. She slaved away at that job. She would work a full day at Heironimus and then go and clean that beauty shop. You would think that her two damn-near-grown sons would have gone in there to help her, but we seldom did. She did a lot to be sure that we were properly cared for during my senior year.

The summer before my senior year in high school, my brother and I went to D.C. and spent time with my dad, as we normally would. This particular year was important because as a senior, I was expected to attend Captain's Practice. During Captain's Practice, the team would primarily just lift weights, and quarterbacks, running backs, and receivers would run through plays together. I skipped the practice my junior year, but this year was different because as a senior, and being one of the leaders on the team, it would have been good for me to be there.

Because I missed Captain's Practice the summer of my senior year, the coaches did not select me as one of the team captains. I understood why and didn't sweat it.

I had a good senior year. I was selected as player of the week on both offense and defense in one game. It was cool because

I received both Offensive and Defensive Player of the Game against Cave Spring.

you got a free meal at McDonald's, so I received two free meals. Although we went two and six, I made First Team All-Metro for the second year and First Team All-Timesland. I never had much time to relax after football season because I had to be at basketball practice within a few days. It was always difficult because of all the nagging minor injuries, such as slightly pulled muscles or sprained ankles that never had a chance to completely heal.

We had a great basketball team my senior year. Ricky led the team that year with a twenty-three-point-per-game average. Watching Ricky play was like poetry in motion. He won the Most Valuable Player in the State All-Star Game. I was the starting point guard. We lost the second game of the year, and we didn't lose any more games until we lost in the regional playoffs. We finished the season at twenty-two and two.

All of the athletes from Fleming and PH hung out together. We would always go to Stanton Park to play basketball, and on one particular day, most of the best athletes in the city were there. Cheatwood, Mark Grogan, Tony Baison from Fleming, Mickey, and the Hardy Twins from William Byrd, Ricky, Keith Wyans, and me from PH. We were playing one game after another for most of the day.

We would play from sunup to sundown. Normally we would get some beer after playing, but that day when we got to the store, we probably had only four dollars between us. Somebody asked one of the girls that we knew for her change when she came out of the store. Then somebody else asked another person for their change when they came out of the store, and I said this is what we're going to do. We asked everybody that came out of the store, especially the girls, for their change. I was the ring-leader, so it was decided that I would keep the money.

Now, it's important to note that in this small town, you had the best athletes in the city in front of this store asking people for money as they would come up. I think we may have gotten twenty or thirty dollars, that was more than enough to buy two cases of beer. That's what our lives were like at that point in time in terms of the camaraderie, the friendship that we shared, and that bond.

I graduated from high school at eighteen. I was 435 out of 437 in my class. My mother was elated. My father was there, Will was there, but again, I wasn't really a family guy. I couldn't wait to just get with my friends and go hang out and get drunk.

Although, I do remember my dad had a pink Cadillac. He got a new car every two or three years because he always leased the car. We went down to my grandmother's house and Dad gave me the car, and I went and got Ansley and we went up to Mill Mountain. There's a star on a mountain, that's why Roanoke is called "Star City of the South." We hung out and had a great time. Then I took her home and got Eric, and we went and hung out.

Everything in my life from high school until I was about thirty-six years old involved alcohol. I always had a beer in my hand.

I had met a recruiter from Virginia State, Mr. Golden, in the gym at school and talked to him about playing football in college. I think he may have said something during that conversation like, "You don't have to have a particular GPA to go to Virginia State." Or maybe he said something about a 1.9. I don't remember, one of the two. I applied to Virginia State University and was accepted.

Five

First Generation

VIRGINIA STATE UNIVERSITY

Virginia State University is one of 110 Historically Black Colleges and Universities or HBCUs, as they are commonly known. This designation means that these institutions were established in the 1800s primarily for Black students because they were not allowed to attend White colleges. Today, as it was then, regardless of one's race, creed, or color, any student can attend an HBCU.

I worked out twice a day for a few months before school was to start. My goal was to play football at State. I was buffed because I had been training hard. I was recruited by some other schools, but I didn't want to play for them. I wasn't recruited by State, but I was planning to walk on.

I took a Greyhound bus to Virginia State University for orientation. The campus was buzzing with people everywhere... Black people. After noticing practically everyone on campus was Black, I noticed the girls. It was a hot summer day, probably 90 degrees. The girls were walking around in shorts and tank tops. I rushed to check into my dorm room. I wasn't sure who my roommate was going to be yet, but I didn't care. I dropped my bags and immediately went back outside. I wanted to get back out there and see all of those beautiful girls.

A couple of my friends from Roanoke were there for orientation. We all went to the freshman orientation assembly together. During the assembly, they did this chant that every VSU student knows: "All the Trojans want to hump, de dump, de

35

dump," and next thing I knew I was up dancing. Everybody was screaming. Though I remember one or two people from home that were there, for the most part I didn't know anybody, but I still thought I was the man. I'm was dancing, and already, within hours of the orientation, I was starting to get a little rep.

Also during orientation, there was a basketball game between the freshman. The gym was packed. I was picked to play. Ten guys took their shirts off; the other guys kept their shirts on. I was on the skins, so I took my shirt off, and girls were saying, "Whoa," because I was so buff. I was saying to myself, "Okay, this is cool. I'm liking this."

I was showing off and had a great game. Now I had a little reputation around the school. People were starting to know me and speak to me. That's when I met Patrice Morris. I saw this girl from New York with a long ponytail, great body, beautiful—keep in mind that up to this point I had only introduced myself to girls over the phone. I'm like, "What the hell am I going to do now? How am I going to work this out?" I don't remember exactly how it happened, but I introduced myself to Patrice, and we connected. For the next three months, every night, I sat in that damn Byrd Hall, her dorm lobby, talking to her, wondering when we were going to at least kiss.

Orientation went great. At that time, State conducted four orientations, and I had such a great time during my orientation that I stayed for the next one. I didn't even go home. I ended up staying in Eric's room. State told me that I couldn't stay for another orientation, and I said, "Watch me." I thought, who's going to know? I went through the second one, and I did the exact same thing that I did in the first, showing off my dancing during the "All the Trojans want to hump de dump de dump." This was the life!

MY ATHLETIC CAREER ENDS

I went home after the orientations and continued to train to walk on for the football team at State. Tom Brown played football for State, and we were good friends. Tom lived in Roanoke. I told him I wanted to walk on and that I wanted to go with him when he went back to State for spring practice. He agreed to let me ride with him. We went down and stayed in the dorm with a couple of the other players because we didn't really have a place to stay. We were there with these other players, and Tom started smoking a joint, and they were passing it around. Later that day, one of the coaches came and said that the entire team had to move to the stadium, and we all got kicked out of the dorm because we were smoking reefer. We had to go stay in rooms under the stadium. It was damp and cold, even though it was summer. It was just the worst possible place to sleep, and everybody was angry with Tom and me.

It was time to go work out. We started jogging around the stadium. It was damn near a hundred degrees. In my high school, we never ran. Our coach believed that you would get in shape just running plays in practice. We ran around that field, and I damn near fell out. This was not what I anticipated at all. I told Tom, "I don't know if I can do this." But Tom said, "You can do it. You'll be all right, just hang in there." I managed to make it through the next few days. Finally, we went back home again because school hadn't started yet. By that point, I was agonizing over whether I wanted to go back and try to walk on. I told Tom I didn't know if I wanted to play football anymore. I didn't know if I wanted to go back to Virginia State. I finally decided that I wasn't going back to State with Tom. I wrote him a letter and left it on his car. I wrote, "Tom, by the time you read this letter, I'll be with Ansley, and I'm not going back." Tom said that when he got the letter, all he did was laugh. I didn't realize how impactful that decision would be or how it would affect me because I had been playing football since I was eight years old.

It was time for school to start, so I packed my things, and Eric and I rode down together. Yes, after spending much of our teens as friends, we were now not only going to be attending the same college, but we were going to be roommates. We ended up staying in Langston Hall in room zero. A lot of people remembered me from orientation, so it didn't feel that far removed from high school in terms of the level of popularity I had. Some people might go to college and feel somewhat out of place. I didn't feel like that at all. It did take me a while to learn how to meet girls on campus because my high school technique didn't go over well in college since I wasn't playing football.

That said, my first year in college was not what I was used to athletically. It was different sitting in the stands, watching the team play and not being out there. But truth be told, I had sustained several injuries from all those years of playing football. I'd had two concussions, a separated shoulder, cracked ribs, and countless pulled hamstrings. I didn't miss playing as much as I thought I would. Then, too, I played intramural football, so that made up for some of it.

PARTY PHI PARTY

At State, as at many other HBCUs, you have fraternities, and you have what are called social organizations. A social organization is recognized by the institution, but it's not considered a member of the National Pan-Hellenic Council or the "Divine Nine," the Black Greek Fraternities and Sororities. A lot of people from Roanoke had gone to State and belonged to an organization called Party Phi Party. Seven of us decided to pledge Party Phi Party, including Eric. Five of us were from Roanoke. Three brothers that pledged us were from Roanoke: Darnell and Daryl Woods, as well as Tom. It was tough being pledged by brothers that knew you and that came from your same hometown. It was a different experience, but it brought us together as brothers.

Pledging a social organization is just like pledging a fraternity. I will never forget when as I was painting a garbage can in the organization's colors, my father showed up on campus for the first and only time. He told me, "I didn't pay all this money for you to come here and paint trash cans." I didn't say it, but I felt like saying, "You didn't pay a damn dime anyway."

While we were pledging, you're not supposed to shower, shave, or get a haircut for the whole six weeks. After being on line for two weeks, I was not going to walk around campus without a haircut. It was a vanity issue. I went to the barber and got my haircut. We used to wear skullcaps. One night we were over one of the big brother's apartments, and we had to take our skullcaps off, and one of the Big Brothers said, "Rob what the hell are you doing? Why did you get your haircut?"

Looking as serious as I possibly could, I said, "Big Brother, I had tatta (lice), and the doctor told me I needed to get my hair cut." My father always used to say, "Boy, you are always lying." I was a consummate liar. The ability to lie convincingly has always been a skill of mine. I lied to my father so much that I think he went to his grave thinking I was a habitual liar, a cheat, and a drug addict. That's all he saw. But then, up until the time that he died, that's all I was.

More than anything else, lying was a defense mechanism for me. I would use it as a means to escape my reality, to circumvent some undesired outcome, or to achieve a desired end. I can give you an excellent example. I was sitting in my advisor, Dr. Jones', office, my sophomore year. We were deciding what class I would be taking that upcoming semester. My first year in college, I had approximately a 3.3 GPA, but I had failed remedial math both semesters my freshman year. I saw this form in my folder on Dr. Jones' desk that says I have not passed this remedial math class. When Dr. Jones stood up to get a form out of a file cabinet, I grabbed the remedial math form and put it in my shirt, hoping that he wouldn't see this form saying that I flunked this math class two times and that I would have to take it again. It worked, and I never had to take that math class again. I guess Dr. Jones either never saw the form or just assumed I had passed the math class.

The thing that was most important to me that first year in college was to demonstrate that I was not dumb. From the time I was a child, I always had this insecurity about not being smart. So when I ended up with a 3.3 GPA average my freshman year, for a kid with a 1.9 GPA coming out of high school, it was quite an accomplishment. I proved that I could do the work, though I was still struggling with Math and English. My major was Sociology. Having my best friend Eric there as my roommate also helped a lot.

But one of the things that helped the most to sustain me was that my grandmother sent me a ten-dollar money order every week. She was a maid, who made less than a hundred dollars a week. She had to catch several buses to go get that money order and send it to me, but she did that my entire freshman year. I truly looked forward to receiving that money order. I would go to the store and buy myself a quart of beer, a sandwich, a little pack of cookies, and some milk. Eric always complained about it because I had all this old milk in the window from weeks before because I wouldn't drink the entire carton.

Another thing we used to do in college was call "twenty-four." If somebody said, "twenty-four," that meant everyone would stay up all night. It seems silly now, but we truly got to know each other well during these twenty-four-hour sessions. We talked about everything—our families, politics, sports—and of course, we talked about girls.

We played backgammon day and night. I remember this one incident where I was gambling with a student from down the hall. We may have been betting four dollars. We were playing, and I was starting to lose. Eric was standing behind me. He had a side bet. The guy I was playing with was one or two rolls of the dice away from winning, and my last four dollars was on this board.

Before my last roll, I looked around. There were two people in the room that were friends of the student I was playing with, and then me and Eric. He rolled the exact number he needed to roll to win the game. I looked at Eric and at the student I was playing with, briefly glanced at the other two students in the room, put the dice down, and said, "I can't lose my last four dollars," and picked my money up. Eric grabbed his money, too, and we walked out. As we're walking down the hall, Eric said, "I don't know what you were thinking about, but I had two of them. You were going to have to take out a third, but I'm glad that you picked your money up because I don't know what we would have done the rest of the week without this money." Those guys never forgot that we walked out. They were like quasi gangsters and, again, I'm not that confrontational, but I wasn't about to lose my last four dollars.

After finishing my freshman year, I went home and worked at the pool. It was fun for the most part because I was there with most of my friends. Coming home from our first year of college, Eric and I had increased in popularity significantly because we were college students at an HBCU.

THE BROTHERHOOD

When I returned to State my sophomore year, most of us who came from fairly rural areas had taken personality cues from groups of students from either New York, D.C., or Philadelphia. Probably because I had spent so much time in D.C. and Maryland over the summers all my life, I gravitated to the guys from D.C. I liked their style, their swag. I had got a haircut with a part like theirs, just off the center of the middle of my head. It was a big thing back then to have Bass Weejuns. Bass Weejuns are penny loafers, and they were not complete without having a penny in each loafer. D.C. guys also often wore pressed jeans with a white shirt.

That year, one of the guys in particular was extremely well dressed. His name was Chuck. There was a period in time that cowboy gear was fashionable. I will never forget Chuck walking across campus with his cowboy hat and boots. I imitated his style. I bought these wing tip shoes, some pants, and a jacket, as well as a cowboy hat and a bolo tie.

As I said, during my freshman year I played intramural sports. All of the fraternities and sororities and the social organizations like Party Phi Party played one another. We rarely beat the fraternities, but they had a chance to see what a decent athlete I was and how I could play basketball. Darrell Smith was a member of one of the most popular fraternities, Tri T (Tri Theta). One day early in my sophomore year, I was sitting in front of the cafeteria with some other friends, and Darrell walked up and said, "Yo, what's your name, man?" I told him, and he said, "Man, you're going to be a Tri Theta. I know for a fact you're going to pledge, and you're going to pledge Tri Theta." I was like, "Yeah, whatever." But from that point on, I started watching the Tri Thetas.

I had started to take an interest in the Tri Thetas even before Darrell made those comments to me. The year that I got to State, the brothers on the '78 line were just so on point. I mean, they were baldheaded, they were cool, they could step, and all the women loved them. Every time they would come around, the girls would scream. They just carried themselves in a certain way. I just gravitated toward the Tri Thetas.

In late September of my sophomore year, the Tri Thetas organized what they call an interest group meeting. Everybody who was interested in joining the fraternity went to this meeting. There were probably forty or fifty students in this interest group. We were upstairs in the student center called Foster Hall. It was a hot, sweltering room because there was no air conditioning. The Tri Thetas entered the room wearing suits and carrying brief cases, and I just admired them so much. They started talking about what it takes to be a Tri Theta and what the requirements were to be in the interest group. I'm thinking to myself, "Yeah, I'm down. I'm going to do this."

We ended up meeting later that night to formulate the Tri Theta interest group because one of the biggest things that you had to do as a part of the organization was raise money that the line needed to buy different things. We sold hotdogs; we had parties; we did a number of different things to raise money. I always remembered that before I made line, I felt like I was in this fairly precarious state. I hadn't made the line, yet I was being asked to do all of these different things that took up a fair amount of my time. There were about forty Tri Ts on campus, and you had to visit each individual brother to do an interview. More often than not, you'd visit them in their room and just talk about who you were and why you were interested in being a Tri Theta.

A couple of those visits stand out in my memory. For example, I remember visiting Milton Chavis and Dewayne Adams. Milton was the president of the chapter at that time, and Adam was the Director of Song and Step. I remember visiting their room and how clean it was. During my visit, they talked about the principles of Tri Theta and what the fraternity stood for. They gave me a perspective that I hadn't necessarily thought about because I thought of the Tri Thetas as imitating these nasty dogs that can step, and that's what originally attracted me most to the fraternity. But they showed me a different side, talking about the Four Cardinal Principles of Manhood, Scholarship, Perseverance, and Uplift. Milton and Dewayne personified those principles. I also remember visiting Steve Johnson. Steve was what was referred to as the Honcho, or president, of his line. He was pretty much the soul of the fraternity. Steve was a very wise brother, and he also talked about the importance of Tri Theta to the community, and the importance of understanding that this was not a fraternity that you joined solely because you wanted to step and sleep with women. You had to be dedicated to do the work of the fraternity. I visited most of the forty brothers who were on campus, but those three visits stood out the most.

With each visit that I made, I became that much more committed to pledging. Now, again, I had just pledged Party Phi Party that previous year. There were several brothers that pledged Party Phi Party and then went on to pledge Tri Theta because you can pledge a social organization and a fraternity. For some reason, I felt like I was betraying the brothers of Party, but with each day that passed, I wanted to become a Tri Theta that much more.

The pledge period went on for six weeks, and it was getting closer and closer to the time that they were going to take the vote and decide who was going to make line. I was getting anxious because it was getting to be pretty serious. Finally, the brothers called a meeting of the interest group sometime in February, and they told us to be in our rooms on this particular day and time. They were basically telling us that they were going to come and get the brothers who had made line. I remember how anxious I was, just waiting there in my room and wondering, not knowing what the next few weeks were going to be like if I made line.

I was scared beyond belief. Granted, I had already pledged once before, but when you're in that situation, your imagination can truly get the best of you. I was sitting there going through a range of emotions, thinking about all the things that I had gone through over the last few months or so getting to this point. It had been a lesson in life to an extent because there are often times that you experience hardships to achieve a goal without any guarantee of success. At this point, minutes away from knowing if I had made line, all I could do was hope and pray. Finally, there was a knock at the door. I was so nervous my roommate had to open the door. One of the Tri Thetas stepped just inside the door and threw a sealed envelope at me and left without a word. My hands were shaking, I was sweating profusely, and I could feel my heart pounding. I started to hyperventilate. I opened the letter and read the first word: Congratulations. It was then that I was able to breath normally. I read on: "You have been selected to become a Member of the 1980 Nu Nu Pledge Club of Tri Theta Fraternity, Inc." I was overwhelmed with a range of emotions, including joy, fear, and anxiety, but I didn't have time to process what I was feeling. I had fifteen minutes to get dressed and meet in one of the other interest group member's room.

At long last, after months of uncertainty, at least now I knew that I had made line. Now that uncertainty gave way to fear because I didn't know what was about to happen over the next few days, weeks, and months. I went over to this room where they told me to go, and I saw all these other brothers in there that were in the interest group. There were nine of us: Tri T 1, Kenny Lawrence; Tri T 2, Milton Robinson; Tri T 3, me; Tri T 4, William Gordner; Tri T 5, Cedric Donnett; Tri T 6, Pete Ford; Tri T 7, Tony McGriff; Tri T 8, Floyd Miller; and Tri T 9, Anthony Elliot. We were told to go get our fatigues, which became our pledging uniform, and meet back at a certain location. I won't go into too much detail because obviously this part is very ritualistic and secretive. The most significant thing that happened was that they selected me to be the Honcho, which is the president of the line. The Honcho has a fair amount of responsibilities, and I guess the only practical reason that they selected me was because I had pledged once before.

We called the area in front of Virginia Hall, which was the Administrative Building, the Block. That's where the fraternities and sororities performed their step shows. When we went on the block that first night, it was like we were in another world. It was so crowded that we could barely get on the block. I knew from that night forward that my life would never be the same, and it wasn't.

As a Honcho, one of your primary responsibilities is to tell your line brothers where they need to go and what they need to do every morning. I never really had any problems. The biggest thing that we had to do in the morning was to wake the big brothers up. Some brothers were more difficult to wake up than others, but things just seemed to work out fine.

During the initiation process, we participated in the Tri T Roundup. There are twelve districts in Tri T. We were in the third district, which included Virginia State University, Howard University, Hampton University, Virginia Union University, Norfolk State University, Virginia Commonwealth University, University of Virginia, and a few other schools from D.C. and Virginia. Every year, the lines from each school would go to a particular location and compete in a history test, a basketball competition, and a step competition.

This particular year, the competition was at the University of Virginia in Charlottesville. We were all excited about going to the Tri T Roundup. Being probably the best basketball player on my line and always wanting to look good, I was not going to a play in a basketball competition without having some new sneakers. I don't remember where I got the money from, but I went out and bought myself a brand new pair of Beta high tops.

Now you may say, well, what does that matter? Well, Beta had a purple V-shaped logo, and Tri Ts pledges are not supposed to wear anything, I mean *anything*, purple. I had purple on my shoes and a Party Phi Party brand on my arm, which meant that I had pledged before. It was like going into a lion's den. I was fresh meat wearing my purple sneakers with a brand on my arm.

The basketball competition was first. I think we played Virginia Union first, and they only had two players. We played them two on two, and we beat them. Then we played Howard. Now Howard has always been known for having extremely large lines. Howard probably had 15 to 20 brothers on their line. We were standing there getting ready to go onto the court, and the brothers from other schools were in our faces.

One brother happened to look down at my feet, and said, "Are you f...ing kidding me? What the hell are you doing with these purple shoes on?" I didn't say anything. Then we turned around to go into the court, and I heard, "Oh, hell no," and "This f...ing Tri T has a brand on his arm." The brothers from other Chapters came over and began to push me around, until the brothers from my Chapter yelled, "Get the hell off the line!" Mercifully, it was time to go out on the court.

The game started, and I was killing them. I mean, I was killing them. It was a little bitty court, not a full basketball court. It was roughly three quarters the size of a regulation court, and I was stepping a few feet across half court and just firing it up and making basket after basket. I was hitting everything. If you're ever having any problems, the ability to demonstrate a certain level of sports acumen cures a lot of ills. The brothers just forgot all about the purple sneakers and my brand. We were going back and forth. They would hit a bucket, then we'd come down and hit a bucket. We'd go up one, they'd go up one. When there were about fifteen seconds left in the game, I drove down and passed it to Ant, one of my line brothers, and he got fouled. He went to the line and made the two shots. We were up one. They came down and got fouled and got two shots. We were up two at that point.

The Tri T from Zeta Pi Chapter hit one and missed the second. We got the ball, then the buzzer went off, and everybody went crazy because we won. I was also told I had scored the most points ever in a Tri T Roundup. We are still really close to the brothers from Howard who participated in the Tri T Round Up, and every time we get together, we reminisce about it.

Now when it came time to step, we were very good, but that night, Howard was great. They did a step called "Retrospect." Again, if you have that many brothers, you really don't have to be that good, but they had that many brothers, *and* they were that good. They ended up winning the step competition. I think we came in second. As far as the history tests went, the fraternity was founded at Howard, so there is no way in hell we were going to beat Howard on a history test, and we didn't, especially with me because I didn't know a lot of the history. I knew a little bit, but nine times out of ten, when we were studying, we had been up all night, and the last thing I was thinking about was a damn history test.

That was our Tri T Roundup. All in all, we were pretty proud of ourselves because we did in fact win the basketball championship.

I was in ROTC before being initiated into Tri Theta. During the initiation period, I rarely went to class. This was a point in time when there were no wars going on, so being in the ROTC wasn't that serious. The thing that attracted me the most is that you got a hundred dollars a month if you were in ROTC. I was clearly not one of the more serious cadets. I only wore the uniform to get my check. You had to report to the ROTC building and say the only words that were music to my ears, "Cadet Mason reporting for pay, sir," so I could get my hundred dollars. My uniform was wrinkled. My boots weren't shined, but I couldn't care less about any of that. All I wanted was that hundred dollars. One day shortly after the initiation period ended, the Sergeant Major called me into his office and said with a heavy southern drawl, "Cadet Mason, I need to see you. Son, out of this entire semester you may have actually been to one or two classes. It seems like the only time you can show up is the first day of the month when it's time to get paid." He went on to say almost gleefully, "Cadet Mason, you're just not military material, son." I knew he was right, and I really didn't want to be in ROTC anyway, but I was sure going to miss that hundred dollars.

The other significant thing that happened my sophomore year was that I started dating Catrice. She was a cheerleader. She was extremely attractive—bow legged, light skinned, with long red hair. She was probably the first woman that I ever fell in love with. We would do a step on a block that goes:

I want to see my sweet honey baby.

I want to take these chains off and run.

I want to see my sweet honey baby,
Because pledging Tri Theta ain't a bit of fun.

Now, keep in mind, this is what I was singing:

Hold it steady right there while I hit it
Because I reckon that ought to get it.
Working for Tri Theta
Working for Tri Theta
Still got so very far to go.

Somehow during the course of doing this step, I hollered out, "Catrice, I miss you!" The brothers never let me forget that, and they would see me walking across campus, holding her hand. As I mentioned, other than proms, I rarely dated in high school. But this relationship was different. I had fallen in love.

NASTY NEOTERIC NINE

I know I keep saying that I felt like I was "The Man," and now I'm going to start talking about how our line was all this and that, but it's true. We had people that could sing. We had people that could step. We had comics, and we used to do this number called "Hit It" on the block, which is basically a comedy show. Pretty much everyone on the campus got to know us and embraced us. We became rock stars on the campus. We became known for stepping. We officially became members of the Tri Theta Fraternity on March 22, 1980 at 11:30 p.m.

Shortly after being initiated into the Chapter, we held elections for the Chapter Officers. I was elected Director of Song and Step, which meant I was primarily responsible for creating steps for the Chapter. Number nine on my line, Ant, was named the Assistant Director. He definitely should have been the Director because I was not one to create a step. Ant created steps that are still used today by the Tri Thetas at Virginia State.

49

Our Chapter of Tri Theta is widely known for our decorative brands and because we have so many. For example, I have twenty brands, and that's fairly normal for our Chapter. Finally, we became known because we could sing. When you combine those three things, it's pretty powerful when you're putting on a step show, and it didn't hurt that we were fairly decent-looking brothers. In that regard, we were not your typical Tri Thetas. We believed that there was something special about us.

I don't know much about other fraternities and sororities and how they pledge, but Tri Thetas were fairly well known for being physical with their pledges. But we weren't pledged that way, and we didn't pledge brothers that we brought into the Chapter that way, either. We were much more cerebral. We spent far more time talking to them. The line we were most responsible for was in 1982. We talked to them about life and what it's like as a Tri Theta, and how purple and gold can distort one's reality.

We explained to them that sometimes when people see you as a Tri Theta, it doesn't matter the person that you actually are because they have this preconceived notion of who they believe you are. In the same way that we had to visit brothers that wanted to become a part of the Chapter, prospective members had to come visit us. I used to always say to these brothers in the Interest Group that Tri Theta should not be this force that builds character or establishes your character: it should enhance your character. Now we had brothers, of course, that got lost in this thing called Tri Theta and couldn't handle the attention. You have no idea how brutal the brothers were to each other verbally, and if you were not your own man, you could easily get caught up in it, and it could have a deleterious effect.

I lived the life of a celebrity as it relates to that world. There were times back then when we would spontaneously put on a show. Tony would begin to sing. Then we would begin to harmonize behind him. Then we would start stepping, and people, mostly girls, would come flooding out their dorms. The older brothers would hear about it and get upset. They would just say, "You guys think you're super Tri Thetas, yada, yada, yada." Then we started to visit other campuses, and we would step. I mean, I would put on step shows by myself, or sometimes it would just be William and me. We became best friends. If you saw one of us, you saw the other. Eventually, we sort of got used to the notoriety we were experiencing from the campus community and settled down a bit and just basked in the glow of Tri Theta.

There were some extremely bright brothers on my line, which made it somewhat difficult for me because again, I didn't think of myself as a scholar. I didn't think of myself as bright. We would have discussions, and I'd always be apprehensive about the point that I was trying to make because I just didn't feel like I could compare or compete with them intellectually. I didn't feel like I could measure up to these brothers, but they respected me to no end. One, because I was their Honcho; and two, because of my ability to step. There were those brothers that handled the business of the Chapter, but Ant's and my responsibility was to be the showmen on the block and advertise our parties.

For example, we would be in meetings, and we would be talking about these serious issues, what the Chapter needs to do in the community, and I would raise my hand, and I would half-jokingly ask, "Brother Basileus, can we just get a keg?" That was my sole motivation—getting drunk and trying to sleep with as many girls as possible.

That's just the type of person that I was in my early twenties. I felt as if the entire world revolved around me. I was extremely narcissistic and cared little about other people. I operated solely on the pleasure principle.

I've come to the conclusion that this sense of entitlement originated from my mother. Through no fault of her own, she fostered this temperament by buying my brother and me practically everything we asked for. As a result, I didn't learn self-discipline and the importance of delayed gratification that comes with not being given everything you ask for. Both delayed gratification and self-discipline are imperatives for a healthy sociological development.

TRI THETA NATIONAL STEP CHAMPIONS

I went back to State for my junior year. It was the first year that I moved off campus. It was a little place on St. Andrews Street not far from school. It was just a little larger than a closet. Every inch of my bedroom wall was covered with an emblem of Tri Theta, or a Tri Theta poster, or something Tri Theta-related that I had drawn.

Being a junior and fairly well established on campus, I was looking forward to my junior year. As I mentioned earlier, I had been selected as the Director of Song and Step, but one of my Line Brothers, Ant Man, was the primary innovator. He was the one that came up with the steps. Once he had created a step, he would show it to me, and I would do it and make it my own. He would then teach it to the rest of the Brothers.

Every two years the district held a step competition, and the Third District Step Competition took place my junior year in my hometown of Roanoke, VA. The winner of that competition would go to our Conclave that was going to be held in Miami that year. Ant put together the show. We had always been known for stepping, but we were also known for not necessarily being traditional Tri Thetas. We didn't wear gold boots. We didn't wear dog collars. That's just not how we envisioned ourselves. More often than not, we would step in Stacy Adams, tuxedo pants, a tuxedo shirt, and a bow tie. The brothers would oftentimes say, "Here come those Kappa Tri Thetas."

The previous year, we lost the Third District Competition to Tau Beta Epsilon Chapter of Hampton University, and that did not go over well. We were extremely disheartened and disappointed. That competition was held in Richmond, and again, when you think about Tri Thetas, stepping is huge, and at this point we were

1981 District Step Champions from left to right: Robert Mason, Barry Wells, Mark Green, Anthony Elliott, Dallas Lee, William Gordner, Tony McGriff, Milton Robinson, Randy Willis.

still not recognized nationally or even regionally to any great extent. After that loss, I remember Ant saying he was going to come up with a new show. The idea was that if you blinked, you would miss something, and that was the show that he created for the competition that was going to be held in Roanoke.

Fast forward back to '82. We were getting ready for the Third District Competition, which was being held in Roanoke that year. We spent a great deal of time perfecting that show. There were some grueling practices, including a lot of arguments that almost came to blows. Once we settled on who would be on the team, we made the final preparations to leave for Roanoke.

Roanoke is a three-hour drive from Virginia State. Milton and I rode with Pete in his '69 Ford Mustang. Now, bear in mind, this is '82. Pete had a red '69 mustang. His car would stop every thirty or forty miles. Of the hundred and eighty miles to Roanoke from State, we must have pushed that Mustang ninety miles, but we made it.

There were four teams in the competition. We were focused and determined to win. We did something that had become a trademark of a Nu Nu Step Show: before going on stage, as we entered the staging area, we sang a melody called "We Are On Our Way," off the stage, but where people could hear us. Without fail, they started cheering and screaming. When we actually stepped out onto the stage and put on our show, we were going from one step to another with the precision and timing of a well-oiled machine. We won the competition. But this was just the beginning of our journey. The ultimate objective was to win the Conclave in Miami that summer. That was the Crown Jewel.

Within weeks of our victory in Roanoke, it was time to prepare for Miami. The brothers spent a lot of time trying to decide who would go to Miami to represent us. More importantly, we had to figure out how we were going to get there. We didn't really have any money. I think I may have had a hundred dollars at most. There was a brother named Mark Green who was on the step team. Mark was not necessarily one of the better steppers. Things got to a point where Ant was trying to put Mark off of the step team, but it turns out that we were glad he didn't because Mark's girlfriend Cookie had a pool house in Miami, and we ended up staying in it while we were there. So now we didn't have to worry about a place to stay. It was just a matter of getting to there.

We pooled together what little money we had to make that trip to Miami. It was me, William Gordner, Varis Monroe, Anthony Elliott, Milton Robinson, Mike Brown, and Mark Green. We rented two cars and drove down. It was my first time ever going South. As a matter of fact, up until that point, I don't think that I had ever been anywhere other than Virginia, D.C., and New York. We ended up getting lost, and a drive that should have taken ten hours took us fifteen hours.

Having seven brothers cooped up in a fairly small pool house was a little nerve-wracking. Brothers almost started to fight a couple of different times. Somehow, a fire was started. I don't know if we were cooking something or what happened, but a fire started. Cookie's parents were really cool, and they ended up letting us throw a party. All these people came over, but I really wasn't concerned about the girls that were there because at that point, my girlfriend Catrice was there, and having her there with me in Miami was really special.

We practiced quite a bit getting ready for the show, and the day finally came for the competition. I don't necessarily remember being nervous. I mean, we had practiced so much and done enough step shows that I really wasn't nervous. There were three teams in the competition. I don't remember where the others were from. We did what we normally do. In the outer area, we sang "We're on Our Way."

We're on our way to Tri T land.

We're on our way to Tri T land.

When we came out, we tore it up. We put on a great show, and we won. We became the 1982 National Step Champions. That was the starting point for us going from a local Chapter known primarily within the Virginia and D.C. area to being recognized as a regional, national, and then international Chapter. For the rest of that summer, we just reveled in the fact that we had won the National Championship. It was the first time that the Chapter had ever won that honor.

The other significant thing that happened my junior year was that after about a year or so with Catrice, as usual, I screwed it up. I ended up sleeping with one of her best friends, Donna. Donna was the Head Majorette for the band. She had this great body and a beautiful face. I don't know how we started talking, but I ended up going over to her place one night. She fixed two steaks and one thing led to another and somehow Catrice found out. It was the worst few months because that's when I realized how much I truly loved Catrice. She lived in a little place right off campus that had five or six rooms in this long, trailer-like dorm, and I used to go over there and hide behind a tree, or there was an empty room that I used to sit in, and just cry. I just wanted to be as close to her as I could. Then she ended up dating this other guy, and that just made it that much worse. It took me a really long time to get over Catrice, but eventually, I started to feel better about things.

It was during this period between my junior and senior year of college that I really started to go through a bit of a transformation. I had started to think much more seriously about my future and what I was going to do after I graduated. I'd become far more serious about my studies. I was transitioning from what I considered to be a "Tri Theta Dog" into a Tri Theta Man. I'm not sure what gave impetus to this change. I started to read more. I wanted to do all that I could to enhance my vocabulary. I was making a concerted effort to learn new words and to engage in debates when, previously, I would shy away from them.

It was in my senior year of college that some other brothers and I began to wear suits. Tri Thetas traditionally cultivated a nasty Tri Theta dog persona, wearing gold boots, baggy jeans, Tri Theta shirts, and various paraphernalia, but I was about as far from that as one could be. In addition, I had lost the desire to step and to do the things that had defined my existence as a Tri Theta for the past few years. The reason that we wore suits to school was because my line brother, William Gordner, found a thrift shop in Petersburg, and he came home one day with two or three of what we would call "old man suits" that he had found there. I don't know if they were tailor-made necessarily, but they were extremely well-made. From that day forward, we would all pillage every thrift shop in Petersburg and the surrounding area. We would buy suits, topcoats, and pants, and that became the norm for Tri Theta. We could buy a suit for ten or fifteen dollars, and by the time that I left Virginia State, I probably had seven or eight of them, which is a hell of a lot of suits for an undergraduate. People also knew me for my habit of not wearing socks. This started because every time I would go to the laundry, I would lose a sock. It got to the point where I was so frustrated that I kept losing a sock that I just stopped wearing them, even with my suits. I became known as that Tri Theta that never wears socks. If you listen to my convocation speech, you'll hear me say to the Rector at one point that I have socks on.

In my final year of college, two people in particular influenced my life at that time. One was Silvia Bonds, and the other was Ebony Wallace. These were the two women that I was dating basically at the same time. I graduated largely due to the fact that I could focus on my studies because I spent time with them rather than being out partying.

I wasn't hanging around with the brothers. I had truly committed myself to my studies. It wasn't because I was necessarily thinking about graduate school or about getting a job. I just wanted to do better in school. I became far more philosophical about life in general. I mean, I've always been fairly cerebral, even as a teenager, and I definitely was during the pledge period, but I became even more so in my senior year. There was so much that was going on inside of me. I didn't like who I had become, and I was going to make a concerted effort to change it. I had been an athlete for much of my life, and that wasn't my identity anymore. As a result of the beer drinking in college, I had gained a fair amount of weight. Since my sophomore year, I hadn't been taking care of myself. But when I reached my senior year, all of that changed. I started wearing primarily suits or sweaters, slacks, and Stacy Adams. I had a black pair and a brown pair. I was going through a transformation not just physically, but emotionally and psychologically.

I was making all these changes in my life as a senior, and starting to get good grades, and I was starting to think about graduation. A lot of the people around me had graduated. I got to Virginia State in '78, and I didn't actually graduate until '84. As you can imagine, most of the people that I had come in with had graduated and left. At that point, I was still living on St. Andrews Street, and I was having a rough time paying rent. I was hiding from the landlord and stealing cable from the neighbors, but somehow, I muddled through. William, my line brother, and I were closer than ever, and I think William had a lot to do with my mindset changing and my starting to think more seriously about my future. William was very grounded, very goal-oriented, and very career-minded. He was in an Urban Planning program that was fairly new at Virginia State, and the students in this program received full scholarships. If he graduated from the program, he was automatically admitted to the Master's Program at Morgan State. William had a profound effect on my life. There's a book called *The We in Me* that talks about how we take on the personas of the different people we meet throughout our life and William was definitely a positive influence that resulted in me wanting to become a better person.

By this time, the landlord from St. Andrews Street had finally caught up with me and evicted me. I moved to Halcom Manor with another brother named Cornel. He was a graduate student on a fellowship. He was a great guy. I lived with him for about four months until I graduated.

Most people are excited about graduation, but it was one of the most disappointing times in my life. For one thing, I owed Cornel two months rent, and I kept thinking that my dad would give me some graduation money and I would be able to pay him off. I felt bad about the fact that I hadn't paid him in a couple months.

I was at Janice's apartment the morning of graduation when my family arrived. Janice and I had been seeing each other for a few months. She will always have a special place in my life. Other than my family, she loved me more than any woman ever has, and for some reason unknown to me, she was the person I took for granted the most.

My mother, Mammaw, father, and brother came to State for the graduation ceremony. I was glad to see everyone. I was the first one in my family to graduate from college, so obviously they were extremely excited. I went through the graduation ceremony, and I stepped with the brothers on the block. Mark and I celebrated the fact that we had graduated. Believe it or not, Eric also graduated at the same time that we did. We'd been together for ages. But my father didn't give me any money. I don't think he even gave me a graduation present, and obviously my mom and grandmother didn't give me any money either because they didn't have it to give.

Virginia State University Graduation, 1984.

Robert Mason, Jackie Lucas Henderson, and Eric Johnson graduate from Virginia State University in 1984.

Six

The Reality of Life

Once my family left, I was faced with the stark reality that I did not have the money to pay rent after making countless promises to Cornel that I would do so after graduation. Obviously, our relationship was extremely strained. I kept telling him that I'd be able to get some money to pay him. I also kept telling him that I was going to move out. I wasn't working. I would just be there eating his food while he went to work. It was early summer in Petersburg, Virginia, and it was damn near a hundred degrees, so I would turn the air conditioner on while Cornel was gone and try to make sure that I turned it off before he got back home. One day, I neglected to turn the air conditioner off before he got home. As soon as he walked in the apartment, he turned the air conditioner off, and I could hear him walking towards my room. Finally, he had enough. He said, "Rob, I'm sorry, but you are going to have to leave. I've done all that I can do." I could clearly see that he was more disappointed in me rather than angry.

What was I going to do? I couldn't go back to Roanoke. At that time, Eric was living across the street with his girlfriend. I told him what had happened. Eric said he was going to D.C. the next day. I decided to call Nate Jones. He had pledged Tri Theta at Howard the same time that I was on line at State. He was one of the brothers on the line that participated in the Tri T Roundup. I had visited Howard several times while I was at State, and that's how I got to know Nate and several of his line brothers. Our lines were always very close. I called Nate and explained that I was coming to D.C. to look for work. I asked if I could stay with him for a while until I could get situated. He said, "Sure, come on up." So I packed up what few things I had and rode to D.C. with Eric and Jake Sims.

Nate, who was originally from New Jersey, lived in a studio apartment in a row house. When I walked in, the kitchen was to the right, the bed was to the left. There were some shelves that separated the two parts of the room, and that was it. Nate was something like a hoarder. Something took up practically every space in that little room. The idea was to stay with Nate a few months while I found a place and a job. I slept on the kitchen floor. Nate did everything he could to help me. In all, I think I may have stayed there maybe three or four months.

The frat house was three doors down from Nate's house, so I would go there regularly. At that point in my life, I felt extremely empty and lost. I was twenty-six, unemployed, and broke. Most of my peers were just so far ahead of me. Many of them had graduated and gone on to start careers. I felt like my life had stagnated. If anything, I was moving backwards. I mean, I had this college degree, but what did it mean at that point? I was sleeping on Nate's floor and not sure what was going to happen next.

I ended up getting a job with the Peter Hart Research Firm, which was a polling firm. I worked there for a while. I remember applying for a job at Howard as an Admissions Counselor, but I didn't even get a reply. I guess the fact that I would be interested in working in admissions was a sign of things to come, since now I own a tech company where over a quarter million students have completed the CBCA to apply to college.

During the entire time that I was in D.C., I never saw my father. I never made an attempt to go by his house. I lived a very meager existence. It was a tough time. I remember going to some type of festival in the park and being so hungry that I almost ate a Big Mac out of the trash. I had hit rock bottom. Not having any money, I sold the only possession I had that was of any value: my fraternity shield I had made while I was at State. One Saturday, I was at the Frat House with Walter P. Patterson. We called him Walter P. He was a district, or regional, officer in the fraternity. Walter P. loved my Chapter. He was one of the judges in Miami when we won the Conclave. He always talked about how we would sing before we started stepping. Walter P.'s favorite phrase was "pig-f...ers." He would say, "I loved yawl pig-f....ers". We were watching a football game, and I was telling Walter P. how difficult things were and that I didn't have a job. I asked if he would be interested in buying my shield. He said, "Yes, and we will hang it here in the Frat House, and when you are ready, you can buy it back." I guess Walter P. knew how desperate I was. He gave me twenty-five dollars for it. Although that shield was sacred to me, I had to sell it, that's just the state that I was in at that time.

It was late fall, and it was just so unbearably cold sleeping on Nate's floor. I finally decided that I couldn't make in it in D.C. I ended up going back to Virginia State and applying to graduate school. I got accepted, and within a matter of days, I had a room to live in. I still felt just as empty as I had a Nate's. I was drinking heavily at this point. As soon as I got into the dorm and got a little financial aid money, the first thing I did was to go and buy a case of beer. I was in graduate school, but I didn't feel any sense of accomplishment.

I only stayed in school for a semester, and I spent that time drinking and missing class. After the semester I had to move out of the dorm. A fraternity brother named Marshall Nelson let me move in with him. He lived in a two-story, high-end townhouse apartment called Ivy Gates. I wasn't employed, and I'm not sure exactly why Marshall decided to let me stay with him, but he did. While I was staying with Marshall, Reginald Goodwin, we call him Toot, asked if I would be interested in working with him.

Toot managed a shoe store. I forget the name of the store, but he said, "If you want to work, I can hire you."

I only worked at the shoe store for a few weeks. Again, I was just in a really bad place at this time. I'm a people person, so I didn't have any real problem selling shoes, but I couldn't figure out how to work the damn cash register. I just got so frustrated, and it didn't help that I was in a place mentally where I didn't necessarily want to be. At this point, Marshall is looking at me like, "Hey man, you got to pay the rent." I was already a month behind.

I got a part-time job in a clothing store selling suits. I was truly excited about the job at first because I was very fashion-conscious. But again, I don't think I stayed there more than a month. At this point, it was getting close to summer. I'm fairly good with making crafts, and I had all this time on my hands because I wasn't working. I decided to make some fraternity shields that I would take to Philadelphia to the Greek Picnic. My idea was to make the shields and sell them at the picnic. The Greek Picnic was held in Grant Park in Philadelphia. Members of fraternities and sororities from around the world would attend this event. I sold a few of the shields, but it wasn't enough to pay Marshall for a month's rent.

THE ORIGIN OF THE COMMON BLACK COLLEGE APPLICATION

By this time, just like Cornel before him, Marshall was growing more frustrated with me not being able to pay the rent. One day I was on campus, and I heard someone yell my name. I turned around, and it was Erskine Morgan, also known as "Hollywood." I had pledged Hollywood while he was at Hampton University. At the time, he was working for the Office of Admissions at Elizabeth City State University, and he was in Petersburg for a college fair. We went to shoot some pool, and I asked him what he was doing in Petersburg. He answered, "I'm here doing some recruiting." I asked, "What do you mean recruiting? What does that mean?" Hollywood explained, "I work for Elizabeth City in their Admissions Office, and I'm here recruiting students." I told him I thought that was pretty cool. He continued, "Absolutely. I get to travel on the school's dime, and I drive a school car. They fly me around to different cities. They give me a per diem, so it's cool." I was more than just curious at this point. I desperately wanted to hear more. I asked if he thought I could do the same thing and recruit for Virginia State. He told me to go by the Admissions Office and see if they were looking for somebody or if they were hiring.

I had never been in the Admissions Office my entire time at State. I had to ask where the office was. I went there the next day and spoke to the Director of Admissions, Mr. Edward Golden. He was the same person I had talked to about Virginia State in Roanoke, when I was a high school senior. Mr. Golden was a very distinguished gentlemen, small in stature, and very refined. He was a Virginia State graduate and very pro Virginia State. Ms. Irvington was the Assistant Director of Admissions. Although they weren't married, they acted like an old married couple. I introduced myself and told Mr. Golden and Ms. Irvington that I was a recent graduate of Virginia State, that I had a friend who worked in admissions, and that I was interested in seeing if there were any employment opportunities in the office. They said that there weren't, so I told them I'd be interested in volunteering, if that was possible.

I was a decent-looking kid, and I guess they figured I could represent the school well, so they said sure and told me to come back Monday. I was excited. I mean, granted, I wasn't getting paid, but I wasn't doing anything else, and this was as close as I'd ever been to being a professional.

I showed up that Monday, and Mr. Golden introduced me to the office staff. Gary Knight was next door to me. Loni, who was a part of the support staff, had her desk just outside my office. They showed me what I would be doing in terms of how to read student files to determine if they were admissible to the University, where to locate transcripts in the file cabinet, and how to use the copier and printers. It was an interesting time. As I became acclimated, I began to go out with Gary and Aleah, who was one of the other Admissions Counselors, to different recruitment events. One of the first ones I went to was with Aleah. She was polished, articulate, and well-read. She was a consummate socialite who exuded confidence as she gave her presentation.

We were at a recruitment visit at one of the local high schools in the surrounding area. There were a couple of other recruiters there, and we all had to introduce ourselves. A couple of the other recruiters were asked to say few words, then Aleah spoke. I was just incredibly nervous. At this point, I hadn't really been out on any recruitment activities. The only real training they had done was to show me how to look at a student's transcript and test scores to see if they were admissible. One of the responsibilities that you have as a recruiter, obviously, is that you give presentations to try to convince students to attend Virginia State, but I didn't really have a lot of experience with public speaking. That was a fairly daunting experience, and it took some time for me to get over the anxiety of speaking in public.

I would go on to work in admissions for years, and to the extent that I could, I would avoid having to make presentations. This was a bit problematic, since that's one of the primary responsibilities of a college recruiter. There was another point in time where I was asked to draft a recruitment letter that would go out to students, introducing myself as a Virginia State recruiter. I wrote this letter, and I let Aleah read it. I knew from the look on her face when she had finished reading that letter that it was far less than what she had anticipated. I happened to overhear her telling someone, "Robert can't write." I mean, it was elementary stuff I had a problem with, like subject-verb agreement.

Due to my scores on the placement test during orientation at State, I had had to take remedial writing courses. Much of what

I wrote in college, I practically plagiarized. Aleah read the letter and was amazed that my writing skills were so poor. She went on to talk about the importance of being able to write if you were going to accomplish anything in life. That stayed with me even to this day. I'm still fairly self-conscious when I have to write something. I'm a little better now, though I am far from being a good writer.

After about a month on the job, Mr. Golden called me down to his office. Mrs. Irvington was also there. Mr. Golden said, "Robert you've done a good job thus far, so we're going to offer you a full-time position as an Admissions Counselor." I was absolutely elated. I don't think they knew what they were getting themselves into, but at that point in my life, it was one of the best things that could have happened to me. This was the starting point, my first introduction to the world of admissions, and it laid the groundwork to the establishment of the CBCA. I went back to Marshall and told him that I had gotten this position, and of course he was excited because he felt like now, I'd be in a position to pay rent.

Most colleges look for fairly recent graduates to work in their admissions office because typically they are the most enthusiastic about encouraging new students to attend. They also have timely, accurate and germane information about the university they attended. It is for these reasons, I guess, that Ms. Irvington and Mr. Golden decided to give me the job.

THE LIFE OF AN HBCU RECRUITER

It was September and the start of the new recruitment season. A typical recruitment season for a college or university runs from September until about March. Kraft Foods was sponsoring a series of college fairs. It was called the Kraft HBCU College Fair. They brought together HBCU representatives from across the country to do fairs in different cities. Mr. Golden and Ms. Irvington allowed me to go on this trip. The tour was going to start in Detroit.

Mrs. Irvington made the airline reservation and booked the hotel reservations because I didn't know how to do so. I had never flown before. I don't remember what the per diem was at that point. I think I was going to be gone about a week, maybe a little longer, so they gave me approximately three hundred dollars. I was nervous and excited. I'd never been anywhere other than New York, Virginia, D.C., and Miami. I was going to be flying for the first time. Mr. Golden brought me to the Richmond Airport and put me on the flight. I was a little nervous. I remember there was some turbulence, but all in all it wasn't a bad flight.

When I first got to Detroit, I was just amazed to be in a city that I'd never been in before. I had to catch a taxi to the hotel. We stayed in a circular hotel on the river, right across from Canada. It was called the Renaissance Center then. It was something like fifty stories high. I was a kid from the Projects who had never stayed in a hotel in his life. I walked into this hotel and was amazed. I didn't act like it, though, because that's just not who I am. I checked in and caught the elevator up to the 55th floor. When I opened the door and walked into the room, I was amazed. I had this panoramic view of the water and Canada. I was thinking, this is the life that I want to live.

There's something about HBCU recruiters that you have to know. One, we were all competing against one another in terms of the way that we dressed and how we carried ourselves. A couple of brothers that I met on the tour were really cool. Steve Smith was recruiting for Jackson State University. Steve was also a Tri Theta. Vernon Martin was recruiting for Lincoln University. Craig Grooms was also a Tri Theta and recruited for West Virginia State University. Marshall Rainy represented South Carolina State University, and Dave Anderson represented Hampton University. We became the life of the tour. As we were traveling on the bus, we would bribe the bus driver to stop by the liquor store so that we could all get some alcohol. We became extremely close over the years. We would work college fairs in each city where we would see thousands of students during the day and party the night away. The next morning, we had to be back at work. Keep in mind, we were dragging all of these boxes of brochures around because that's what we were giving out at the college fair. Before the fairs, we would have to check in. There were long lines of tables like you would see at an expo. There were reps from probably about forty colleges there. It was like nothing that I had ever seen before. There were fifteen or sixteen high schools in the Detroit Public School system. They would bus the students from all of these high schools into the civic center in downtown Detroit. Thousands of students would attend these fairs. The fair started at nine o'clock in the morning and ran until about two o'clock in the afternoon, and during that time you would have waves of high school seniors coming into the venue. We worked frantically, handing out cards, trying to answer questions, and giving out brochures. Virginia State was probably not extremely popular in Detroit, but because there were so many students there, all the schools were seeing large numbers of students. I thought it was great because I wasn't giving presentations. I was just answering questions and handing out brochures. It got to the point where there was finally a lapse and the waves of students finally stopped. At the end of each day, I went back to the hotel to relax. Later, I would meet with some of the other recruiters to go to dinner. We ended up doing that every night. Afterwards, we would go to these different clubs. All of us drank, me probably more than the others.

We had a great time. At that point in time, Detroit had a great nightlife. We would get back to the hotel at two or three in the morning, and the fair would start again the next morning at nine. We would all be hung over, and we were all running late. We'd go to our tables and do the same thing that we did the day before. We weren't nearly as enthusiastic as we had been on the first day. I was hardly answering any questions at that point. I was just handing out cards for students to complete. Students were trying to get information about Virginia State, and I would just say, "Please just complete the card and we'll send you the information." The students would leave the table extremely frustrated. At the end of the fair, we would all go back to the hotel and crash. Then we'd get up and do the same thing all over again later that night. It got to the point we became so close that we started to call ourselves The Breakfast Club.

When the fairs were over, I went back to Petersburg, and things were fairly uneventful. I had been in the office now for two or three months, and I had developed a routine. I may have gone to some different high schools to do some visits, but one of the things I had not done was stop drinking. I was still going to the pub on campus, and between the pub and hanging out in the local clubs on weekends, I was constantly coming into the office hungover. I definitely came in hungover on Monday mornings. Loni would say, "Oh Robert, you smell like beer again. You stink." I would be like, "Loni, shut the hell up."

My co-worker Gary was a big brother, a father, a counselor, and a teacher to me. He was from a small town just outside of Petersburg, and he came from a fairly big family. He was a light-skinned, good-looking guy. He was married with a beautiful family, and he just took me under his wing. I was far from being the model employee. In fact, I was absolutely the worst employee a person could be.

I remember Mr. Golden telling me one time, "Robert, you're just like a cow. You fill up the bucket with milk, and then you kick it over." After about six months, I was starting to show up to work late more often and missing college fairs. I remember one time in particular I was so hung over that when the university president came up to the Admissions Office to talk to Loni and somebody else, I was literally throwing up in the trash can at the same time that the president was just outside my office.

On countless occasions, Gary offered me the advice that a big brother or a father would offer. Gary was a model employee.

69

He was conscientious. He was always at work on time. He was always dressed professionally, and he was extremely enthusiastic about the University. I was none of those things. At Virginia State they had state cars for the recruiters, and they would give me a state credit card to use to put gas in the car. These county stores would allow me to buy beer with the state card. I was just abusing the system to no end. There were a couple other times that I had to participate in college fairs in different parts of the country, and I would spend the per diem before I left Petersburg. The drinking, and the less than exemplary behaviors like abusing the credit cards, coming late to work, and missing college fairs, got worse as time went on, and they became more frequent. Mr. Golden retired after I had been in the office for about a year and half. That was pivotal moment in my life because when Mr. Golden retired, they hired a woman named Allison Chambers. Allison was from the University of Virginia. She was heavyset with jeri curls and glasses.

By this time, I was once again in a place where I was starting to think that there was more to life. I was spending time, especially during the summer, in my office that faced someone else's backyard. I would look out the window and think to myself, is this it? Is this all there is? Is this what my life has come to? There's a sign in Petersburg just before you get on Interstate 85 that says Atlanta on it. I used to always look at that sign and wonder what it would be like to live in Atlanta. Granted, I would travel to other places periodically for my job, but those trips were few and far between.

Not only was I still drinking beer heavily, I had started to use cocaine quite a bit. Ironically, around the same time, I think because I had gotten a job, my father was starting to see me as becoming fairly responsible. He bought me a car, a Maxima, and the plan was for me to pay him back. Of course, that never happened. The car had some scratches on it, and it would shut off if the air conditioner stayed on too long. But the one thing that was really cool about the car was that it would talk to you. For example, if you opened the door, it would say "left door ajar" or "right door ajar," and that was pretty cool.

GO STRAIGHT TO JAIL

Allison wanted me to go to Roanoke, my hometown, to do a college fair. As usual, I spent much of the per diem as soon as I got the money. But now I was beginning to spend the money on beer and cocaine. A really good friend of mine knew someone that sold drugs, so I ended up buying a gram of cocaine before leaving to go home to work the college fair. Although I was home, I was staying at the Marriott Hotel. I had been drinking and getting high all day. I mean all day, and a gram of cocaine is a lot for one person. It was probably ten or eleven at night, and I decided to go out for a drive. I don't even know where I was going, but I was going down Orange Avenue, one of the main streets in Roanoke, and these red lights came on. I'm like, "Ah, hell, what am I going to do now?" because not only was I drunk, but I still had a fair amount of cocaine left. I don't know to this day where that cocaine was. I know I didn't throw it out of the car. It couldn't have been in my pockets because the police officer would have found it when they searched me.

The police officer pulled me over. He had me do the breathalyzer and walk a straight line. Obviously, I failed all of the sobriety tests miserably. The officer said, "We're going to have to place you under arrest. Do you have somebody to come get your car?" I don't remember what happened to the car because again, it was a state car. I ended up getting locked up in Roanoke City Jail.

It seemed so surreal that after all the things that I'd been through at home, that I would come back to do some recruiting for Virginia State and end up locked up. Just imagine if I had gotten caught with that cocaine in a state car, it would've been far worse than it actually was. The only thing I remember about being arrested was the sense of confinement. I remember I kept telling the police officer that I needed to get out to go use the bathroom. He said in a dismissive tone, "No, there's a toilet right inside your cell." I said, "I can't use that! I need to get out!"

The officer said, "Sir, you are locked up. This is jail. You can't just go. You don't have that freedom. That's why they call it jail. You can't just go where you want to go." Finally, the realization set in that I was in jail, and I went to sleep. When I woke up the next morning, they let me go on my own recognizance. I went to get the car from the impound and went back to my hotel. My family never knew anything about it. I ended up having to go back to Roanoke to go to court, and I don't know what I told my mom about the whole situation, but in Virginia, at that time, when you got a DUI you had to take a number of classes that reminded me of an encounter group. After I completed the classes, I returned to court, and the judge ordered me to pay a thousand-dollar fine and suspended my license.

When I got back to Petersburg and walked into the office, Allison had this sheepish grin on her face. I knew something was going on. Gary called me into his office and said, "You're in trouble, Slice." Slice is what Gary called me. It turns out that Allison had gotten copies of my credit card statement, and she had seen where I had made all of these fraudulent charges buying cases of beer. There were a number of different things that she could have done, but what she did was call the campus police and tell them what was going on. I was fired on the spot, and Allison took my keys to the office and asked me to leave. When I was on the way out, I remember her saying something to the effect that the police would be coming to my apartment to arrest me. Sitting there when I got home, waiting to see what was going to happen, was one of the most frightening times in my life. By that time, I was no longer living with Marshall. I was staying with a Fraternity Brother named Carlos Cunningham.

Carlos, or Los, was about 6'3" and had played football for Wake Forest University. He was always well-dressed and took great pride in his appearance. Los and I were extremely close. Every Thursday we would go to a club called the Down Under in the Holiday Inn. We had some great times together, but as usual I abused his friendship.

I got a phone call. It was the VP of Admissions asking me to come to his house to instruct me as to what I needed to do to avoid being arrested. When I got there, he said to me, "Look, obviously you're not going to be able to keep your job, but I've talked to the Chief of Police, and basically you're just going to write a letter of contrition. You'll have to resign, and that'll be it." At that point, I was willing to do whatever I had to do to put this entire incident behind me.

I wrote that letter of contrition. I was still fairly worried for a while, but that letter was enough to keep me from being incarcerated, and the school didn't press any charges. Looking back, again, it seems like all of this was a divine intervention because if all of this hadn't happened, I may not have left the state when I did, and if I hadn't left, I definitely would not have gone on to create the Common Black College Application and affect the lives of hundreds of thousands of students.

Months before being fired from Virginia State, I had applied to Graduate School at Atlanta University and had been accepted. At the time, it was Atlanta University. It would not become Clark Atlanta University until the next year when Clark College and Atlanta University merged. This was probably early summer and by this point, Carlos had pretty much said to me, "Rob, you have to go," because again, I wasn't paying any rent.

For a while, I was sleeping on different fraternity brothers' floors. I'm sure the brothers would hate to see me coming. The brothers had meal cards. You could get the main meal and you could get seconds, and I would always ask them if I could get their seconds. I never knew where I was going to be staying. I was basically homeless. There was no one to call. My family was not in a position to help me. By then, my car had been repossessed. I felt such an extreme sense of loss.

Because of the ticket I had gotten in Roanoke for driving while intoxicated, I had started going to these classes. They weren't Alcoholic Anonymous classes, these were state-run intervention sessions where you would sit in a circle and talk about your problems. These were run by some organization affiliated with the Department of Motor Vehicles. As I was taking these classes, I began to realize that I had a problem, and I had to confront it. At that point, I hadn't had anything to drink since I got that DUI.

GOING TO AA

Once I had completed those classes, someone suggested that I go to Alcoholics Anonymous. It might've been somebody in one of those groups that I was in. By now, I was staying with a brother named Tracy Johnson because by sleeping around on brothers' floors, I had found out Tracy didn't have a roommate, so he let me stay with him. I found out there was an AA class that I could walk to from Tracy's place, so I went to a meeting.

I didn't know what to expect, but I had nowhere to go but up. I was just trying to get my life together and honestly, I don't even know if I was making a concerted effort to do that. It's just that something compelled me, and I knew that going to AA was the right thing to do.

The first meeting I attended was in a smoke-filled room in the basement of this church. It seemed like everyone who was there chain-smoked and drank coffee. We sat in a circle, and it started off like you've seen on television: Hello. My name is Rob. I'm an alcoholic. People shared their stories, I was just sitting there, listening. I was just enthralled by the stories that they were telling and the level of hardship and the things that these people had had to endure. That particular night, I didn't say anything. As I was walking home, I was thinking about what I had just experienced. AA says you need to change people and places, but I think the thing that helped me the most was that from that point on, any time that I thought about drinking, I thought about God. I'm not sure if this makes any sense to somebody who's not an alcoholic or an addict, but thinking about my spirituality prevented me from drinking, and it was fairly easy for me from that point on.

I think it was probably the next meeting when they asked, "Does anyone else want to share?" that I decided to tell my story. It was one of those surreal moments in which I felt this out-of-body experience instead of being the one actually telling the story. When I finished, I had tears streaming down my face as everyone thanked me for sharing. That was one of the most liberating experiences that I've ever had in my life. I felt like I had been cleansed. I still have my chip to this day that says, "Think before you drink."

Over the next month, I became a regular at the meeting, but it was getting close to September, time for school to start. Mike Irby, another Fraternity brother that I had pledged, was from Georgia. It just so happened that he was driving back to Atlanta, and he agreed to give me a ride. I remember sitting there in the dark at Tracy's house waiting for Mike, with my acceptance letter, my financial aid papers, and five dollars to my name. When I got in the car with Mike and started to drive to Atlanta, I was both figuratively and literally making a change in my life.

ATLANTA UNIVERSITY

It was near midnight when we got to Atlanta, so we stayed at Mike's brother's place with the plan of going on campus the next morning to try to get registered. I had no idea what the future would have in store. All that I owned was in a pillowcase. After talking to Mike and his brother for a while, I finally fell asleep, but it was a restless night.

When we got to Clark Atlanta the next morning, I first went to the registrar's office. I had to meet with my advisor, Dr. Anso. There were some other students in his office as well, and we were all looking around and asking questions. Finally, we introduced ourselves. One brother, Patrick Daniels, and I met in his office. Pat was a Tri Theta as well, so obviously we had a bit of a bond from the start. I was going to be majoring in Public Administration with a minor in Human Resources. In the entire department there may have been forty students. There were only fifteen or twenty students in my class, and we were a fairly close-knit group.

Pat had attended Clark College as an undergraduate. He had a larger-than-life personality. He knew all the brothers and was well-connected. He was extremely smart, very well-read, and articulate.

We went to register for classes in the gym and then to the financial aid office. They looked me up, my financial aid was in order, and I was admitted. The next thing was to find a place to live. They said to go to Ware Hall where the graduate and undergraduate students stayed. During those first few days that I was on campus, there just seemed to be alpha-type personalities everywhere, just big personalities. There was this woman who was in charge of the dorm who was very outspoken, one of those people who wouldn't tolerate any foolishness. I introduced myself to her and told her that I'd been sent down there, and I ended up getting a room in the basement. I was fortunate enough to get a room by myself, so that was pretty cool. Within forty-eight hours of arriving in Atlanta, I was registered as a full-time student, and I had a place to stay. The next challenge would obviously be how I would eat. I didn't get a meal card, so I had to get a job.

On my first day of class, there were maybe ten or fifteen of us all sitting there, and in walks Dr. Onge. He was from Cameroon. He ended up being a mentor, an advisor, and a counselor to all of us. He had this very deliberate way of speaking. I learned so many life lessons from him and the other professors.

I really learned to appreciate him as a teacher. The way he taught me to process information is something that I still use to this day. Always start with the foundation, that is, the reasons why a particular discipline was established. By foundation, I mean

76

what socio-economic and cultural factors gave impetus to that particular thinker? From what need did a particular innovation arise? We all have our own philosophies, and there are factors that contribute to us establishing that particular philosophy. When studying a particular discipline, to this day I always strive to understand the origin of that field of study. After Dr. Onge introduced himself, we got to work right away. I think I took ten or fifteen pages' worth of notes that first day. I was not a scholar by any means, but by this time I had established some solid study habits and developed a bit of confidence, so I was able to perform on a level comparable to other students in the program.

I had one more professor that year, my advisor, Dr. Anzo. I won't say he was an introvert, but he was fairly soft-spoken. He came from a long line of African royalty. He employed teaching methods similar to those of Dr. Onge. His class wasn't quite as interesting because he wasn't quite as animated as Dr. Onge, but I think I took ten or fifteen pages worth of notes in his class as well.

One thing that happened in that first semester that was extremely devastating was that I got a C on one of my first tests. There's no such thing as a C in grad school. A C in grad school is just like an F at every other academic level, and I was distraught. I remember thinking, "Oh my God, I have nowhere to go from here. Did I make a mistake coming to Atlanta? Am I smart enough to do this?" That's about the time when Pat and I really got close, and he comforted me. He said, "Rob, you got this. You can do this." He encouraged me to study harder, and I did. From that point forward, I committed myself. Pat and I continued to grow closer, and I went on to get all As in those three classes.

I secured a work study job in the Clark Atlanta bookstore, and I would often eat lunch and dinner at Bond's, a small convenience store. No matter how little time you spent in Bond's, you would come out smelling like chicken. The chicken wings were the absolute best.

Although I spent most of my time concentrating on my studies, I decided to go out with one of my friends from college, Ernie, who had moved to Atlanta two years before me. Ernie had a little Volkswagen convertible, and we would hang out occasionally. On this particular night, Ernie came to pick me up, and we went to what was then Deion's Club 21. This was where everybody was going, and Ernie and I decided to go. I didn't have very much money because I was only working in the bookstore. We were standing by the bar, and suddenly I saw this girl on the other side of the club. Her name was Tanya Alworth. Tanya had this distinctive look. She was gorgeous. Ernie noticed that I was staring at her and said, "Go introduce yourself to her. She is fine!"

I was still a little reluctant to just approach women. I still am, to some extent. The next thing I know, Ernie went over and started talking to her. Tanya looked at me, and Ernie waved me over. He introduced me to Tanya. She said, "I'm not going to bite you," as she was laughing and reaching out to shake my hand. She immediately put me at ease. We spent the rest of the time dancing and laughing the night away. I spent my last thirty dollars buying Tanya drinks, but I didn't care. Tanya said she had to leave, so I walked her to her car. She was driving a new Mercedes. It turned out that she was married, though separated at the time we met, to a professional football player for the Washington Redskins. Before getting in the car, she gave me a hug and kissed me on the cheek.

We talked on the phone almost daily after that night at the club. Tanya had this voice that was very sensuous and sultry. She invited me to her place one night. I don't remember where it was now, but Ernie let me borrow his car. Tanya lived in what I would consider to be an upper middle-class neighborhood. As I was approaching the house, Tanya walked out and gave me a hug and a long kiss. That was the start of a great evening, and I ended up staying the night.

So there I was, living in a dormitory basement, and I was spending time with somebody like Tanya. As you can imagine, I felt pretty good about things in general. Then one day she called me because she was having some financial problems. She wanted some money. I'm not sure what she needed the money for. I said, "Tanya, I live in a dorm. I'm in graduate school. I don't have any money." At the time I had just gotten a student loan, and I thought about giving her the money, but I decided against it. I told Tanya I didn't have the money. Tanya said fine and hung up. I could tell she was disappointed. I knew I would never hear from her again, and I didn't.

I was still working in the bookstore, but by this time I had only gone on a couple of recruitment trips for Clark Atlanta. Cliff Rawls was the Director of Admissions. I had met Cliff during a conference when I was working in Admissions at Virginia State, and we got along well. I went by his office one day and told him I was in graduate school there. He said he didn't have any positions available, but I told him if he needed me to go on any recruitment trips that I would. Cliff had kept me in mind, so I ended up going on a couple of trips representing what had now become Clark Atlanta University.

GRADUATE SCHOOL INTERNSHIP

The biggest thing that happened during my first year of graduate school was that Chrysler came to interview students from the Business School and from the Public Administration Program for summer internships. It was very competitive. Everybody thought that securing a Chrysler internship would be a great opportunity. Truth be told, I didn't place a lot of significance on it. I also didn't understand the importance of interning with a company like Chrysler and what that could potentially mean. But there was this sign-up sheet to schedule an interview, so I signed the sheet and got a time slot. I didn't think much about it again until I was talking to Pat and he stressed how important it was and what it meant. It wasn't until a day or two before my actual interview that I started to understand the significance of it.

By the time I left for D.C., I had given most of my suits away, so on the day of the interview, I wore the only suit I had left. The Chrysler representative who interviewed me couldn't have been much older than her late twenties. She asked me about the Public Administration Program and about my major. Then she asked me why I was interested in working for Chrysler. After about ten or fifteen minutes, the interview was basically over, and we just had a general conversation. I remember telling Pat afterwards that I thought it had gone extremely well; not because of anything that I said necessarily, but because the recruiter and I connected.

A week or two later, I got a letter saying that I was one of a handful of interviewees who had been selected for the internship. I was pretty amazed, again, because I hadn't placed much emphasis on it or stressed about it. Once it actually happened, though, I was pretty excited. I spent the rest of that spring finishing up my first year of classes and preparing for the internship, which would take place that summer. Summer came, and it was time for me to go to Detroit. Chrysler flew me up, and we stayed on the campus of Lawrence Tech, which was a community college. I had a roommate in a two-bedroom apartment. He was really cool, and we really hit it off. Remember, Detroit was the first city that I flew to when I worked at Virginia State. I have always had an affinity for Detroit, and I still do to this day.

On Monday, I went to the Chrysler headquarters, which at that time was in Highland Park. My experience with the internship reminded me a bit of being in high school because as I've already said, I've always questioned my intelligence, and I have a bit of an inferiority complex as a result of that. Being surrounded by all of these extremely bright people made it a very difficult summer for me. They were accommodating, and they did all that they could to create an environment where I felt comfortable, but at the end of the day, I was there to work, and I wanted to be viewed as competent.

One of the first things that happened was that they gave me a car. Of course, it was a Chrysler. I wasn't necessarily interested in American cars, but if you work for Chrysler, you're going to drive a Chrysler. I was working in the HR Department because Human Resources was my minor. At that time, Chrysler was creating a new benefits package for its professional staff. They were rolling out a new insurance plan with all these different features, and I didn't have a clue as to what was going on.

We would be in meetings discussing the different features of the various benefit plans, and I found myself so totally lost that I didn't even understand much of the terminology that was being used. My anxiety was exacerbated by my belief that everyone could see how unprepared I was because of my inability to contribute in the meetings when I was called upon to give my opinion. When asked, I would just say that I agreed with one of the other members in the meeting. I just didn't have the level of expertise to offer any insight or suggestions concerning whatever topic was being discussed.

The Chrysler staff would always invite me to dinner, and finally I reluctantly accepted because I figured I had to. In corporate America, that's just something that you do. I remember arriving late because I didn't want to be there a for a long time. I just didn't speak the corporate language. I felt out of place and inferior.

I would go to work and figure out a way to get through the first few hours up until lunch. I would eat in my car, and then take a nap. My body shuts down at two o'clock. It always has. I take naps religiously. I would take a nap, wake up, go back to work, and just do whatever I could do to get through the next few hours. Then I would do it all over again the next day.

Now, socially, as far as going out and enjoying the fact that I was in Detroit, I had a ball. I met Jolene Olsen. Jolene had a sister that was married to a player on the Chicago Bull's basketball team. This was at the same time that the Bulls were winning Championships. Up until I met Jolene, I had met a couple of other women in Detroit, and again, I was having a ball going out every weekend and some weeknights. It's amazing, the difference between the two lives I felt like I was living. I was miserable at work, but I was having the time of my life after work.

Jolene and I started to spend a lot of time together, and things were becoming fairly serious. Within weeks, we were practically living together. She had a Pug named Dino that would sleep under the bed and snore louder than anything I had ever heard. The one other thing I remember about Detroit was that it was fairly cold for the summer. I don't think I've ever experienced a summer that cold, but people in Detroit tell you it's fairly common. They always say, "If you don't like the weather, just hang around for a few more minutes, and it'll change," and that's true.

When the internship was about to end, there was a performance review. My manager was as accommodating as he could be, considering that I think we both realized that there was very little chance that Chrysler was going to hire me. I don't remember seeing the work review, but I'm sure it wasn't good. I didn't get hired, and I didn't expect to be hired. It was time for me to go back to Atlanta to finish the second year at Clark Atlanta.

CAU ASSISTANT DIRECTOR OF ADMISSIONS

That summer, after I received my master's degree, a position became available in the Admissions Office, and Cliff gave me a job. I became the Assistant Director of Admissions at Clark Atlanta University. Pauline Winston was the Associate Director. Mrs. Walker was over Operations. Mauline, one of the hardest workers I've ever known, was part of the support staff. The recruiters at the time were Tanya Mitchell and Tracey. We also hired a Tri T Brother named Kelvin Ryles. Kelvin had gone to Tuskegee. All in all, it was a very, very interesting group that worked in that admissions office, but the thing that was the most important to me was that Cliff basically let me travel wherever I wanted to travel because my primary responsibility was to coordinate the recruitment efforts.

I moved out of the dorm and stayed with Ernie and Edward Morgan, whose nickname was Bean. They lived in an apartment about twenty minutes from campus. I had finally gotten my credit in order, and I was able to get a red Miata, a two-seater. For the first time in my life, I had a car that had heat, air conditioning, and music. I loved that little car. Things were going pretty well.

Cliff and I became extremely close. Cliff became a mentor, a big brother, a confidant, and most importantly, a friend. Without Cliff in my life, to a large extent I would have never been in a position to create the CBCA. Cliff believed in me enough to basically turn over the recruitment efforts to me. Although I wasn't drinking and drugging anymore, there was still a part of me that was extremely narcissistic. It was my job to determine what recruiter would go where, and I probably did sixty to seventy percent of the out-of-state travel. Every year for about four years, it was basically the same schedule. I gave them the trips I didn't want to take. I would do all of the major fairs or fairs in cities that I wanted to go to like Chicago, LA, D.C., Detroit, and New York.

I wanted to do those fairs for several different reasons. One, they were fabulous cities where there was always something to do. Two, the per diems were larger. You would get more money going to do a recruitment activity in New York than you would get doing a college fair in Savannah, Georgia. I was getting what was at the time some pretty large per diem checks. I was getting seven hundred to a thousand dollars in a per diem check, which was meant to be used for hotels, travel expenses, and your food. More often than not though, just like at Virginia State, I spent that check before I even left Atlanta.

This went on for a few years. When the new Lexus came out, I used to rent a Lexus in practically every city. I can remember the Accounts Payable Officer at Clark Atlanta asking in disbelief, "Why are you renting a Lexus? Isn't there something else much cheaper that you could be driving?" I simply shrugged my shoulders and went on my way. I was starting to get a reputation as a bit of a snob on the college recruitment circuit. I wasn't riding the bus like everybody else. I was not staying in the recommended hotels because one, I wanted to get points, and two, I liked staying in nicer hotels.

I learned several trade secrets when traveling during those years, for example, how to get a government rate at hotels, how to fly several segments to get more frequent flyer points, and to always use the same hotel chain, airline, and rental car services to gain elite status. For example, if I wanted to go from Chicago to Atlanta and the non-stop fare is $500, if I book a ticket to fly from Chicago to Fort Lauderdale with a change of flights in Atlanta instead, that trip might be half the original cost.

As I indicated previously, I've always been fashion conscious, and I was using some of my per diem checks to buy suits and shoes. There was a bit of a fashion show or a competition of sorts between the HBCU recruiters in terms of who dressed the best. Because we spent so much time together, there was a lot of camaraderie, but there was also a fair amount of hating or shade-throwing that would go on, and a fair amount of it was directed at me. For example, we would go to St. Louis from Detroit. The other recruiters would take this ten-hour bus trip and by the time they got to Detroit, I was sitting in the lobby relaxing and refreshed because it had only taken me an hour or so to fly. You can imagine how they felt about me. It's not that I would bring it up, but as I said, I'm pretty good at showing off, and that was exactly what I was doing.

This went on for about five years, and during that time, Clark Atlanta got a new VP of Student Activities, Dr. Dian Whatley. Our recruitment numbers had started to decline. As a result, Dr.

Whatley ultimately lost confidence in the current management of the Admissions Office. Eventually she pressured Cliff to retire.

When Cliff left, Mrs. Wade took over for a short period until Dr. Whately hired Ms. Cavers as the new Director. I was away on a recruitment trip, and when I came back, there was someone else sitting in Cliff's office. The arrival of Ms. Cavers was another pivotal moment in my life. On that particular day, when I came back off the road, and she was in Cliff's office, I walked in and introduced myself. We started to talk about how much time I was spending on the road, recruiting. I told her that I did much of the out-of-state recruitment, and she said something to the effect of, "That's going to change," in a very condescending tone. And change, it did.

YOU'RE FIRED

A major HBCU college fair was being held in Seattle, and I was there representing Clark Atlanta. There were thousands of students and parents attending the fair. It was a very festive environment. DJs played music, fraternities gave step shows, and sororities and gospel choirs performed. One of the students sang a song, and someone announced, "Congratulations! You've received a full scholarship to Howard University!" Then this high school choir went up on the stage and sang. A female student sang a solo, and she was phenomenal. When she finished, everybody was cheering, and I don't know what came over me. I walked over to the announcer, and although I didn't have the authority to do this at all, I told the announcer that Clark Atlanta was going to offer that student a full scholarship.

The announcer asked the audience for their attention. She brought me up onto the stage and told everyone there that I was from Clark Atlanta and that I was offering the student that had just sang the solo a full scholarship. Again, I just got caught up in the moment. I was feeling pretty good about myself at this point, and I don't think I really worried about it at all because I knew the gospel choir director at Clark Atlanta, and I assumed that this student was talented enough to be offered a scholarship. I clearly didn't think it through.

When I returned from Seattle, days went by. By this time, Ms. Cavers and I were barely speaking to one another, but one day she abruptly called me into her office and asked me, "Mr. Mason, did you promise a student in Seattle a scholarship?" I told her that I did. She wagged her finger disapprovingly at me and said, "Who gave you the authority to do that?" I said, "No one." I think she told me that the cost of the scholarship may have to come out of my salary, I don't remember, but at some point, I walked back to my desk. I do remember calling the Gospel Choir Director and talking to him about it. He told me that he wouldn't be in a position to offer this student a scholarship.

I was starting to realize the gravity of the situation and think that I may have made an irreparable mistake. Ms. Cavers had called the Assistant VP of Student Activities, Dr. Long, and told him what had happened. Dr. Long called me over to his office. I admitted that I had offered the scholarship, and he told me that I didn't have the authority to do that. For the most part, he was pretty cool. But Ms. Cavers wanted me terminated. As a result, Dr. Long sent me a letter saying that I would need to resign by the end of the month, which was a few weeks away.

I wasn't sure how to process all of that. I knew I detested Ms. Cavers. I knew I wasn't going to work there much longer anyway, but when you don't have any options, it can be pretty devastating. During those last few weeks, I continued to show up to work, but the environment had become extremely toxic by that point. She asked me to file some documents, and I refused to do it. I remember telling her that filing documents was not a part of my job description and that her asking me to do so could be perceived as harassment. Yes, I was purposely being sarcastic and insubordinate. She called Dr. Long again and insisted that I leave immediately. Dr. Long told her to let me finish working out my last few weeks, and then I would be gone.

It was sometime during the course of that last few weeks that I woke up at six o'clock in the morning with this idea of creating a service whereby students could use one application to apply to multiple HBCUs at the same time and pay one fee. The next day, I started to work on what would become EDU, Inc., the Common Black College Application.

Seven

Get Educated

THE CBCA TAKES FORM

One of my co-workers, Tanya Mitchell, helped me put together the first paper Common Black College Application. Tanya was like a little sister to me. I called Garrett Drake, the Director of Admissions at Morehouse, and asked, "Could I come your office and talk to you for a second?" He said, "Sure." By then, I had two pamphlets for the CBCA. I explained to him that the CBCA was going to contract with HBCUs to represent them during various marketing and recruitment activities, and the students would be able to use this one application and apply to all CBCA Member Institutions at the same time for one fee.

Drake and I were close because we would always see each other on the road during different HBCU recruitment activities. We had a mutual respect, and I know Drake looked at me like his little brother. I believe that Drake felt the CBCA concept was sound, but I know that the respect we felt for each other was just as important in him in deciding to allow Morehouse to become a CBCA Member Institution.

The next person I spoke to was Steve Smith, a recruiter at Jackson State University. Steve was a part of The Breakfast Club, which was a group of HBCU Recruiters who socialized together on the recruiting trail. Steve and I had grown extremely close over the years. He is also a Tri Theta. As a matter of fact, I'm the godfather to one of his daughters. I called Steve and explained to him what I was trying to do, and he said, "I can't make that decision, but I can put you in touch with Brandice." Darryl Brandice was his Director of Marketing and Recruitment. I met with Brandice to explain to him what I was trying to do, and he said almost immediately after the presentation, "I'm on board." Then I called Mike Taylor. Mike was the Director of Admissions at Lincoln University. Mike is also a Tri Theta. I explained to Mike that I wanted to start this company where students would be able to use one application, pay one fee, and apply to several HBCUs at once. Mike said, "I'm down."

I had the same conversation with Peggy Martin, the Director of Admissions at Florida Memorial University and with Joyce Givens, the Director of Admissions at Savannah State University. Keep in mind, I wasn't charging the schools at this time. Although, as I said, I had a reputation for being arrogant, egotistical, bougie, and whatever else, the recruiters I knew still respected me, and I think that to some extent, that is why these first five schools were willing to be a part of the service.

THE FIRST FIVE MEMBER INSTITUTIONS

My last day at Clark Atlanta was getting closer. I left as unceremoniously as one can possibly depart a job where he or she has worked for five years. There were no parties, no nothing, just get the hell out, primarily because of Ms. Cavers.

I had just started a Ph.D program (which I would not finish) and had gotten a student loan for $8,000. I used much of that money to start the company. I got a P.O. box. The plan was to have students complete the paper CBCA. They would send it in to the P.O. Box that I had just purchased, and I would make copies of each application and send it to all five Member Institutions, and that's what I did for the first year. I got 10,000 copies of the application made, and I thought I was on my way. I thought I was going to make millions.

When September rolled around, I went back out on the road as I always had as a recruiter, but this time I was representing the

CBCA. There were some real challenges that first year. The first city that I went to was Denver. Being on the road representing my own company as opposed to Virginia State or Clark Atlanta meant I needed to significantly alter my travel habits. I had grown accustomed to staying in some of the best hotels and driving these great cars and flying, often in first class, from city to city. But now it was cheap hotels, the cheapest rental car I could get, and the cheapest flights available as I traveled to these different cities. I marketed the CBCA in the same way that I had marketed and recruited students to Clark Atlanta or Virginia State. One of the things I did was to buy a book that was published by the College Board that listed High School Counselors and their mailing addresses. I was trying to create my own database that I could use to mail packets to school counselors nationwide.

SLEEPING ON FLOORS

I was sleeping on floors of friends and Fraternity Brothers while eating fast food for breakfast, lunch, and dinner. At this point, I would be remiss if I were not to take the time to thank three Fraternity Brothers that played a vital role in helping me to establish the CBCA: Corey English in Los Angeles, Carlton Gilbert in D.C., and Nuroh Johns in Chicago. Each of them allowed me to stay with them for weeks at a time when I was in their cities visiting high schools. I would simply call them and say I would be in town, and without hesitation they would open up their homes to me. They never asked me to pay them any money to stay. Corey would even call me and ask when I was going to be in town because over the years, he became familiar enough with my recruitment schedule that he knew the time of year I would be in LA. He teases me to this day about the Coogi sweater I would wear to every high school visit. He called it my "uniform." I owe all of them a sincere debt of gratitude. They believed in my dream of the CBCA becoming a success just as much as I did. It should be noted, all three of them have gone on to become accomplished in their own fields of endeavor. God blesses those that bless others.

Although many college fair organizers allowed me to participate in the fair, there were a significant number that did not. I think the politics of me only representing HBCU's may have had something to do with that.

During a college fair, representatives from various schools would be stationed in the designated area of the school such as the cafeteria or library. When I did a high school visit, I would either set up in the cafeteria, or they would invite students down to come talk to me in their college center. Having one person represent several different colleges was an entirely new concept. To schedule a high school visit, I'd call the high school, ask for the counselor that schedules high school visits, and once I got that person on the phone, I would explain to them who I was and what the CBCA was about. I had been in Admissions by that point for about twelve years, so I knew a fair number of the counselors, and I would call on those with whom I had relationships. They would allow me to visit their high schools primarily because they knew me from being a recruiter at Virginia State or Clark Atlanta. For the most part, schools were willing to let me come in, but some of them did say no. In their defense, I was representing a company with a totally different concept that they had never heard of, and they were simply trying to protect the interests of their students. Some of them probably thought it was a scam, because at that point in time it was fairly uncommon for there to be a fee associated with an educational service, although the fee was only twenty dollars to apply to all five schools.

Progress was slow. I was beginning to wonder if I had made the right choice and if this was something that was going to work. But one of the things that kept me motivated was that whenever I would get to this kind of low point, invariably something would happen that felt like divine intervention.

As an example, I was in Los Angeles, and there was a college fair that was going to be held in San Francisco. My credit cards were overextended, I had a rental car and only twenty dollars in my pocket, and without knowing if I had enough money to make it, I just started driving to San Francisco. Although I was broke, I was still trying to live that high life and impress others. I would rent these humongous mobile phones along with the vehicle. This was years before cell phones were made small enough to fit in the palm of your hand.

I was on my way to San Francisco, and as I was exiting to get on Interstate 405, I called my credit card company, anticipating that my request for an extension would be declined, but I had no other choice. After a few minutes, the credit card representative came back on the phone and said, "Mr. Mason your credit limit has been granted for an additional three hundred dollars." I hung up the phone and literally cried for the next half an hour or so. I just knew that these situations were one of God's ways of saying to me, "Rob, I got you, just keep pushing. Just keep trying to do the right thing. Don't give up." That was a very pivotal moment for me. There have been countless situations similar to this, whereby I know I was touched by God, but truly this was one of those divine moments.

By the time I got back to Atlanta after that tour, I had missed a couple of month's rent on my apartment, and I was starting to get threatening eviction notices. I thought about Ernie. Ernie had bought a house by then, and he was living out in Fayetteville by himself. I called Ernie and asked if I could stay with him. Without hesitation, he said, "Absolutely."

The only thing about it was that Fayetteville was extremely far from the city, but I was left with few options. I brought a leather love seat, a print from a popular artist that I still have to this day, a couple of suits, my computer, and my plants, and I moved in with Ernie.

I agreed that I would pay Ernie $400 a month. I was just coming off of my first year of trying to launch the CBCA, and I had probably made less than $1,000, so I was a bit afraid. I didn't know how I was going to pay him rent.

No matter how dire my circumstances became, though, he never threatened to throw me out. Ernie was an only child, born and raised in a middle-class West Philadelphia neighborhood by his mother Doris Oglesby, a teacher, and his father Ernest Oglesby, who was an entrepreneur. I became extremely close to Ernie's parents. I called them Mr. and Mrs. O. They treated me like a son, and I loved them dearly.

A year or so before starting my company, I had joined a gym called Fitness First. I had become fairly adamant about trying to stay in shape. Although it was getting more difficult to continue my fitness regime, living in Fayetteville and having to drive an hour to go to the gym, I still managed to make it at least a few times a week. Obviously, there were gyms that were closer to where I lived, but a gym is a lot like having a barber or a beautician that you will drive for hours to see. I had several friends that went to Fitness First, and I truly liked the atmosphere.

ERNEST OGLESBY

I moved to Fayetteville with Ernie in July of '90. The gym changed ownership that summer. One day when I was working out, I noticed a sign adverting that they were hiring fitness trainers. As a long-time athlete, I was still in decent shape. I had informally trained friends, but I wasn't certified as a trainer. This gym, which was called Ax Fitness, was fairly new, and they subscribed to a philosophy that I would characterize as pop fitness.

Everything was cutting edge. We even had a full-fledged boxing ring in the gym. I found out that the trainers made pretty decent money, so I applied, and I got the job. They put me through a training period with the idea that while I was working, I would be studying for the test to become a certified trainer.

The gym charged a hundred dollars an hour for training sessions. From the beginning, I decided that I wasn't going to

93

train any men. I would only prospect women because one of the things that we had to do at the end of a session was to take them through a series of stretches, and there was no way in hell that I was going to be stretching out sweaty men after taking them through a workout.

I was extremely successful working for Ax Fitness. I was gregarious, and I had a particular strategy. I would walk the gym floor looking for potential female clients who were already fairly fit and ask, "Have you ever been taken through a training session? You appear to be in really good shape." Most people in a gym adhere to a particular set regimen. When you take them out of their routine, they tire quickly. A lot of these women would say, "Wow, I didn't know I was in such bad shape."

That was a very successful strategy. After taking a potential client through a session, I would stretch them out, and that's when I would pitch her on buying sessions. The sessions were a hundred dollars an hour. I felt it would be difficult to get that much for an hour training session, even in an area as exclusive as Buckhead, so I decided to alter the cost. I offered clients three sessions for that same amount. I might have to spend a bit more time with each client, but I would still make a fair amount of money because out of that hundred dollars, I would get to keep forty.

The head trainer was tracking us, and he was amazed that I was closing all these deals and getting all of these clients. Little did he know, I had reduced the cost of a training package by a third. The clients were still paying the same amount, and the head trainer thought that I was doing things the way that I had been instructed to. The gym was generating money, and so was I. I think I made about ten thousand dollars that summer. That's more money than I had made in two years with the CBCA.

Although physically demanding, working at Ax Fitness as a trainer was a great job. I met some very attractive women. I was training corporate executives, strippers, and Atlanta Falcons

Cheerleaders. But more importantly, I made enough money to get through the next few months.

It got towards the end of the summer, and I was getting ready to go back on the road with the CBCA. When I left, that's when Ax Fitness found out that I had basically been giving sessions away because people were coming in and telling them that the gym still owed them sessions. When the training director found out that I was discounting the packages, he barred me from the gym. I wasn't overly concerned because I didn't plan on coming back.

My car lease was up, and with the money that I made that summer training, I was able to get a new car. That created a bit of a problem with Ernie because at this point I still wasn't paying rent regularly. He once said, "You went out there and got another car, but you're behind on the rent?" We were both fairly fortunate because Ernie's mom basically took care of both of us. She was paying the mortgage until Ernie got a really good job and was able to start paying it himself. She used to come by, and it got to the point that I couldn't face her because she basically knew I didn't have any money and that I wasn't paying any rent. She never said anything, but I'm sure she was thinking that I was able-bodied, I had a college degree; clearly, I could go out there and get a job. I owe Ernie and Mr. and Mrs. O so much because they basically supported me the first few years of the CBCA.

I went back out on the road again that fall, and I was at a high school in Oakland when the school counselor called me into his office and said, "I want you to look at something." It turned out to be the Internet. I didn't realize what this would ultimately mean, but I do remember that was the first time that I became aware of the Internet. By the third year of the CBCA, I had started to learn a bit of HTML in order to create my own website. By that point, I had signed on thirteen schools. I built this really crude website. Back then, everybody was out there trying to build websites. I thought it might be a way for me to generate some additional revenue for the CBCA. I was having a fair amount of success getting more schools to come on board, and around this time I started to charge schools nine hundred dollars to become a Member Institution. Prior to that, the only revenue I had been generating was from the student application fee, and that was not a enough to sustain the company.

Although I had built a crude website, I was still printing applications. I would take the applications to Staples or Office Depot and make copies. Every September, I would go on the road. I would take those applications to a college fair or a high school visit. The students would complete the paper application and give it back to me, or they would mail it back to my P.O. box. Then I would make copies of the application and send them out to the participating schools. I ran the business this way for three years. But sometimes those applications were slow coming back. It was always so disheartening to go to that mail box, time and time again, and not have even one application from a student.

The first few years with the CBCA was a really tough time. It reminded me of when I was pledging. Although, there is no guarantee, there are times when you have to just stay committed and pray for success. Time and again, things would happen that would keep me just motivated enough to continue moving forward. For example, in the second year, I was really wondering if the CBCA was the right thing to do. I reached out to maybe ten more schools at that time, and five of them actually came on board. That reassured me that I had a viable idea.

A COMPANY BY ANY OTHER NAME

The company was incorporated as EDU, Inc. in 1997. When I first started the company, I spent several days deliberating about what I would call it. The first name I thought of was EDU, Inc., because all education-related websites at that time ended with .edu. My rationale was that anytime somebody thought about EDU, they would think about the Common Black College Application. In fact, the CBCA was branded as EDU, Inc. more so than as the Common Black College Application for the first fifteen years.

I also had to decide about the logo. I was reading a magazine, and it had a picture of the silhouette of two male and female figures in an apple. I drew the figures inside of a building steeple and wrote the words "Black College Common Application" on the bottom. "Get Educated" wasn't added until 2007.

One day, I got a cease-and-desist letter from an internationally recognized company, and that's when I knew the CBCA was starting to be recognized as an educational service beyond just those students who had completed the application. The letter said I was going to have to change the name of my company because it too closely resembled the name of this other company. That's when I changed the name from the Black College Common Application to the Common Black College Application.

I was trying to determine how I could generate some revenue to conduct high school visits and participate in college fairs that coming fall. I decided to go to New Jersey and work with one of the brothers that I had pledged, Mark Green. He had started a booking agency called Celebrity Talent, and Mark was looking for some help. I put what few items I had in the Miata and was off to New Jersey. It was a seventeen-hour drive. I had ample time to contemplate what was going on in my life both socially and professionally. The CBCA was beginning to gain some traction, but it wasn't even remotely anywhere near where I had thought it would be by that point. I got to Mark's apartment around one or two in the morning. At the time, Mark lived in Hackensack in a four-story garden-like apartment just off of I-95.

THANK YOU FOR BEING A FRIEND

Mark was much like my mother. He was obsessive compulsive. Everything had to be in its place, and let's just say that I was far less concerned about things like towels being properly placed on a rack, rugs being aligned straight on the floor, and pictures being hung properly. When I walked in, Mark, as always, had a big smile on his face. He was always a well-groomed, good-looking brother and extremely laid back. He had been a trusted friend for years. There was one thing I had always noticed about Mark, though: he was not inclined to loan anyone money. He had no problem paying for dinner when we would go out or buying drinks at a club, but he was far less likely to loan me money. But perhaps that was only with me because he knew I would not be inclined to pay him back.

Mark had a one-bedroom apartment. It was not one of those contemporary places. It had a fairly outdated kitchen. You could stand in the middle of that kitchen and touch both walls on either side. But considering the state that I was in, I was not one to complain. We sat up much of the night talking and catching up. When it was time to go to sleep, I laid down on the couch, which was a little larger than a love seat, and I was squirming. I think Mark had the air on, but it wasn't down extremely low, and it was a humid New Jersey night. I started sweating, trying to sleep on this leather couch. After tossing and turning for a few hours, I ended up just sleeping on the floor. My mind was just racing, thinking about what the future held.

There I was, once again sleeping on a brother's floor, with only a few hundred dollars to my name and most of my earthly belongings in a pillowcase. One of the things I remember most about this time and several other moments during these early years was that I never lost faith in the viability of the CBCA. I absolutely had questions and doubts, but I never gave up. I had experienced so much pain and anguish in my life, much of it self-inflicted, but I just felt in my heart of hearts that God had so much in store for me and that he wouldn't allow my suffering to be in vain. Comforted by that thought, I finally fell asleep.

The next morning, I woke up to the smell of fresh coffee brewing and bacon sizzling. Mark asked if I was hungry and if I drank coffee. "I don't drink coffee, but I'm definitely hungry."

As we ate, we started talking about Celebrity Talent and what I would be doing.

In one way or another, Mark had been in the music business practically all his life. He'd been the road manager for several celebrities, including some of the biggest stars in the business. Recently, I found out he has been credited with being one of the original creators of rap and that he is being included in the Hip Hop Museum. During this period, Mark had just started Celebrity Talent. The furniture in Mark's place was arranged to allow two people to work fairly comfortably. He had a small desk with two chairs and a couple of phones, the couch, and the stereo system all neatly arranged. Mark's place always smelled good. One thing that Mark did that I learned from him and I still maintain to this day is to line up all of my colognes on the bathroom sink. I just liked the way it looked. My brother does the same thing. I guess he got it from me.

Rather than Mark giving me a true orientation, he gave me this book of all these different venues where acts perform and a list of some promoters. He also showed me the list of the talent. They were mostly B- and C-list artists, because A-level artists worked with major booking agencies. I am not one that had any in-depth knowledge about hip hop music. I have a fairly decent knowledge of R&B, and I have almost no knowledge of rap. In order to do this job effectively, I needed to have an in-depth awareness of each artist's recent releases and what was going on in their lives. I knew none of that. I can't even say that I am a real fan of watching the different music award shows. I was probably the least qualified person for this position, but Mark assured me that I could do it. "Just keep making phone calls, and you'll close some deals and make money."

So I started making phone calls, and I was having absolutely no success at all. I was calling different promoters and telling them, "Hello, my name is Robert Mason. I'm with Celebrity Talent. I'm calling to ask if you have any interest in booking any acts." I was repeatedly being told, "No." Those that didn't say no asked me questions that I had no clue how to answer.

We were sitting next to each other at a table and I was trying to ask Mark the questions that I couldn't answer at the same time that he was trying to close a deal with another promoter on his phone. Promoters would say things like, "Tell me what R&B artists you have," and I would begin to name some of the artists on the list. Then the promotor would ask, "Well, what's their latest hit? Are they hot?" I would repeat the question loud enough so that Mark would hear me, and he would write the answer on a notepad, or he would whisper to me what the artist was charging, and I would tell the promoter. Then the promoter would ask, "How many are traveling in the band?" or "Are they using a DAC?" I didn't have a clue as to how to answer any of these questions, so I was just getting more frustrated.

There was one time that a promoter asked me if we could get an A-list artist. I said the artist's name loud enough for Mark to hear me, and he wrote "$100" on the pad. I said, "Yes, we can get them for $100." Mark dropped his phone and started yelling, "No, no, no! Not a hundred dollars!" He jerked the phone from me to tell the promoter that artist they wanted was not a hundred dollars but a hundred thousand dollars. Pointing to the pad, Mark said, "Can't you see that's $100,000?" I said, "Hell no...that looks like three zeros instead of six." Needless to say, we stopped using that strategy where I would try to ask the question I was being asked loud enough for Mark to hear me.

It felt like I made a thousand calls that day. Mark said I only made ten. I didn't even get close to closing a deal. In spite of my glaring mistake, Mark attempted to be as encouraging as possible. "Don't worry about it. You'll get used to it. You'll start to understand, and you'll be able to answer the questions." I replied, "All right, cool."

I shrugged it off, but the next day it was pretty much the same thing. I wasn't learning anything because I wasn't overly interested. I wasn't trying to learn anything. I was trying to take a clinical approach to what I was doing, but Mark was saying, "No, it's not that kind of business. You just have to get in there and study the stuff, look at the different shows, like on BET and MTV." For weeks, I would make calls, and people would ask me the same questions that I couldn't answer, and I was starting to get extremely frustrated.

In addition to working for Mark, one of my reasons for coming to New York was that I wanted to visit high schools while I was there. I had recruited in the New York area when I was with Clark Atlanta, and I knew some school counselors in the area. Counselors that I did not know gave me a more difficult time when I tried to schedule visits because this was in the first couple of years of the CBCA and they were not familiar with the company. Those that were interested enough to ask how it worked would refuse to let me into their schools once I explained to them that students had to pay a one-time fee to apply to all of the CBCA Member Institutions.

A few interesting things did happen during this time. After about three weeks of making calls for Mark, I got a lead. I called this guy up, and we started talking, and he wasn't like most of the other promoters I had spoken to previously. He was in Atlanta, so we started talking about Atlanta, the Falcons, and the Hawks. Mark was listening the entire time, waving his hand in a circle, gesturing for me to stop the small talk and ask the promoter if he is interested in booking any acts for his club. By then, I was finally starting to learn a little about the business, and I was able to answer some of the guy's questions. He said he was interested in an artist. Now I'm waving my hand at Mark trying to let him know that his guy is interested in buying an act. Mark started gesturing for me to give him the phone, and I kept shaking my head. I was determined to close this deal myself. We finally settled on an artist and on an amount, and he asked me to send him a contract.

The contract was for three thousand dollars, and I got a ten percent commission on it. I'll never forget it because that's the only check I received the whole summer. We sent the promoter a contract. He paid the first half up front, and Mark was elated, mostly for me and that I had closed my first deal. He said, "We've got to go out and celebrate. You closed your first deal!" But as I said, it turned out to be my only deal, and I know Mark was disappointed. He had to be because I'm sure he thought that I was going to be able to help. I just wasn't any good at it. It just didn't work out, primarily due to my lack of interest. I have learned that unless I'm committed to what I'm selling, and I believe wholeheartedly in the product or service, it's useless for me to be involved.

My vested interest and genuine concern for students is evident when I begin to talk about the CBCA. There have been several occasions when I have been giving a presentation or in a meeting, and I begin to discuss the CBCA, and when I think about the countless lives we have changed, I become emotional and have to stop the meeting to collect myself. Just recently, I was presenting to a group of educators, and I began crying uncontrollably while telling the story of one student who literally ran down the hall screaming, "I'm going to college!" after receiving an acceptance letter from one of our Member Institutions. My aunt teases me because she has attended several public events at which I have presented, and invariably at some point during the speech, I became emotional.

There is one other unforgettable thing that happened while I was working for Mark. We were making our usual calls. Every now and then we would get a call from a manager who had an artist they were trying to break into the music business. Mark got one of those calls. He asked the manager how much money the artist wanted, and Mark told him he would see what price we could get from the different promoters. Then Mark turned to me and said, "I just got off the phone with a manager, and he has a new artist that he's trying to break." I started making phone calls. The first promoter I called wasn't interested. I called another one, and he wanted to know how much the artist charged. I said $7,500. Then the promoter asked me the same questions we were typically asked, and I tried to answer them. Then Mark's phone rang. He picked it up and said, "Okay, so how much does she want now? Okay. All right, cool." He turned to me and said, "Rob, now she wants $15,000." That can happen because artists can just be that hot that quick.

I started calling more promoters, trying to book the artist for $15,000, and Mark's phone rang again. He said, "Wow. Okay. I'll see what we can do." He hung up and told me that the artist now wanted $30,000. This all happened in less than an hour's time. I will never forget that experience. I literally had a chance to sit there and watch how an artist can blow up in minutes, and it was just so amazing for me to get an insider view on how that part of the music industry works.

I woke up one morning, exhausted from the night before because we had gone out to a club. I turned on the television, and saw that a plane had flown into the World Trade Center. Bear in mind, I am right across the George Washington bridge from Lower Manhattan. I didn't realize—I don't think anybody realized—what had just happened or what was about to happen, and how that day would change so much about our lives. I was pretty much glued to the television all that day. A friend of Mark's named Keith came over later on that afternoon. He was also a member of Tri Theta. We all sat there glued to the television. Even now, I can't adequately describe what I was feeling. Mark lived across the street from an elementary school, and a little later that day, the school bell rang. I'm sure there were kids there whose parents had been in the World Trade Center, and I remember thinking that some of those kids would never see their parents again. That's when I truly began to internalize the severity of the tragedy that had just occurred. Watching it on the television, it didn't seem real. But hearing the school bell ring and thinking about how some of those kids coming out of that building probably wouldn't be able to see their parents again was devastating.

Eight

Love Hurts

I made it a habit to do some high school visits in Philadelphia every September. Hackensack is about an hour and a half from Philly, and I decided to drive down to do a couple of high school visits and a college fair.

I was on my way Philadelphia, and I needed to use the men's room. I took an exit and pulled up to the front of the Adam's Mark Hotel. I told the bellman, "I'm just going to go in for a second, and I'll be right back." He said okay and asked me to leave him my keys. Walking towards the men's room, I passed a line of offices with some open doors. I looked into one of the offices and saw "that face," and something visceral happened. Her name was Gabrielle Sanchez, and she was truly one of the most gorgeous women that I've ever seen in my life. I immediately started to think, "I have to say something to her." I gathered myself and took a couple of deep breaths because I had started to sweat profusely at this point. I walked into her office and said, "Excuse me, can you tell me where the men's room is?"

She looked up, and I was almost speechless at that point. She was just that gorgeous. She had a slender face and long, curly, black hair. She told me the men's room was just around the corner. I thanked her and walked to the men's room. "Wow, okay, what am I going to do? I have to say something," I thought to myself. "I am not leaving this hotel without saying something to her."

I stood there for a few minutes, trying to regain my composure. I forgot all about the fact that I needed to use the men's room. I headed back to her office and walked right in before I had a chance to talk myself out of it. I said, "Excuse me, my name's Rob. I'm in Philadelphia for work, and I don't know anybody here. Do you happen to know of any restaurants or lounges that you would recommend? I'm going to be here for a couple of days."

She suggested Penn's Landing, where there were quite a few restaurants. I said, "Maybe this is a bit presumptuous, but would you be interested in joining me for dinner?" I just knew she was going to say no, or tell me that she had a boyfriend, or that it was probably not a good idea. But she looked up, brushed her hair back from her eyes, and said, "Sure."

I tried not to act too surprised. We made arrangements for me to come back and pick her up around five. My feet did not touch the ground as I left her office and went back to my car. I mean, I literally felt like I was walking on air to think that somebody as attractive as Gabrielle had agreed to go out with me. As I've said before, I never really thought of myself as attractive. I don't think I'm a bad-looking guy because I've dated a fair share of attractive women, but Gabrielle was different. There were so many things rushing through my mind.

I got back in my car and went to do a couple of high school visits. One of the visits was to two of the most renowned high schools in Philadelphia. The schools were across the street from one another. After ringing a bell on an extremely large wooden door, I was let in and instructed to go to the Main Office. I explained why I was there, and I was instructed to have a seat and that the head counselor would see me shortly. The head counselor, Mrs. Chisholm, walked into the office, and the secretary indicated I was there to see her. I stood up and introduced myself, and she asked me to come with her to her office. There, I begin to explain that I represented the Common Black College Application, which allowed students to use a single application to apply to twenty-two HBCUs at the same time for twenty dollars. Normally, when I get to this point in my explanation, if the Counselor begins to nod or make some gesture indicating they disapprove of their students being able to complete the CBCA, they are probably not going to grant my request. That is exactly what happened. Before I had concluded, Mrs. Chisholm interjected and said, "I'm sorry, but we are not going to be able to allow you to see any students because we don't allow students to be charged for educational services like this. And besides, I am not familiar at all with your company."

After being on this high from meeting Gabrielle, the school's refusal to not allow me to meet with their students was disappointing for a number of reasons. The most disturbing reason was that I took Mrs. Chisholm's stinging rejection of the CBCA personally. After a few minutes, I walked over to the other school. That school was perched on a hill, and you had to walk up several steps to get to the main entrance. It was an all girl's school, and there were several students sitting on the front lawn, eating lunch and socializing. There were some students going into the school as I approached the door, so I just followed them in and asked where the Main Office was. I saw a sign on one of the doors, though, that said Guidance Office, so rather than go to the Main Office, I just knocked on that door and was instructed to come in.

I didn't have an appointment, but they didn't appear to be as regimented as the first school. The woman sitting behind the desk politely asked how she could help me. I told her my name and began to explain who I was and why I was there. She immediately responded, "Like the Apply App but for HBCUs?" I felt so relieved to hear that she at least understood the concept of a common application. She went on to say that her name was Dr. Claudet Nelson and that she was the Director of Counseling. Then, almost apologetically, she said she couldn't allow me to see any students because I didn't have an appointment but that I could leave some applications with her. I told her that I certainly understood, and I promised to schedule an appointment the next time. I handed her a stack of about fifty applications, thanked her for her time, and exited the building.

I felt a true sense of accomplishment. This school was arguably one of the better schools in Philadelphia, and to have the head counselor be willing to use the CBCA with her students went a long way towards legitimizing the service. It gave me the confidence to attempt to have the application used in comparable schools throughout the country.

As I got in my car and prepared to leave, my attention once again turned to Gabrielle. By this time it was close to four o'clock, and we were supposed to meet at five. The Adam's Mark Hotel where Gabrielle worked was about half an hour from where I was. I drove back there early and just sat in the parking lot, thinking about this date that I was about to go on. At about quarter to five I walked in, and she was ready to go.

Gabrielle looked absolutely radiant. I mean, she was a model in every sense of the word. She was attractive, she dressed well, and she carried herself like a lady. We rode together, which was cool, and we just really hit it off. It was like we had known each other for years. We just talked about life and our different experiences. What I found interesting was that although at the time Gabrielle was the Assistant Director of Events, she told me that she hadn't gone to college. She had started out working as a secretary at the Adam's Mark and had worked her way up at the hotel, which I thought was extremely admirable. It was different because every woman that I had been with up until then had been college-educated, but the fact that she hadn't been to college didn't affect our budding relationship or my opinion of her in any way.

At the restaurant, Gabrielle told me that she had two children, that she was from Philadelphia, and that her mother had passed away when she was young. I told her a bit about my upbringing. Over the course of dinner, we just connected that much more. At about ten or so, it was time to take her back to her car. I told her that I needed to drive back to New York, and Gabrielle suggested, "There's no real need for you to drive back to New York. I have a big house. If you want, you can stay at my place and sleep on the couch." I was really caught off guard but not overly surprised because again, we really hit it off. With any other woman, at this point, if we had connected to this extent, I automatically would have been thinking about how I was going to sleep with her, but with Gabrielle, it was different. That was the furthest thing from my mind. I just wanted to be around her.

WELCOME TO MY WORLD

As I followed her back to her place, a number of different things ran through my mind. Gabrielle lived in Blackwood, New Jersey. We drove through Philly, onto the interstate, and out to New Jersey, taking these different turns in these residential areas until we pulled into this subdivision. It was a fairly decent subdivision with pretty large houses. Gabrielle took one last right into her driveway. She had an unpaved driveway and a huge house, but it was obvious that the house needed some work.

We both parked, and I started to get a little nervous because I remembered her saying that she had two children, a boy and a girl. I have always been a little reluctant to meet a woman's children because of the way that I was reared and because of my experiences. But I'm good with kids, so I wasn't overly concerned. As we approached the door, I began to hear barking and then I saw her Golden Retriever, Aldo. When Gabrielle and I first started seeing each other, I was not overly enthused about Aldo because he was always present. But by the end of the relationship, I had a love for Aldo that was as great as my love for Gabrielle and the kids. That first night, Aldo came running to the door. He jumped on Gabrielle, circling, barking, his tail wagging. Then he noticed me, and he jumped on me like we had been friends forever. This went on for several minutes. Then Gabrielle's daughter Jonice came walking around the corner, and Gabrielle introduced me.

Jonice and I connected immediately. She had to be probably one of the easiest kids in the world to talk to. She was just so delightful and just as pretty as her mom, with long, flowing hair. We started talking about all kinds of things.

The house was huge and sparsely decorated. There was a table in the dining room and in what I would call the living area. While Gabrielle went upstairs to change, Jonice and I sat at the table talking. Then Kassie came downstairs. Kassie was the grandmother of the kids. Kassie had a heavy Puerto Rican accent, and she was just as warm and inviting as Gabrielle and Jonice. She just had a huge personality. She said, "¿Robert, que paso. Are you hungry?" I was thinking, "Is this real?" It felt as if I was a part of the family.

After about a half an hour, Gabrielle came back downstairs. As she reached the bottom of the steps, the front door opened, and in came Cortez, Gabrielle's son. Jonice was about 12 and Cortez was 15. Gabrielle introduced us by saying we met at her job. I tried to start a conversation with Cortez, but he was a bit more standoffish than Jonice. After a few minutes, Kassie came into the room and said, "Pappi, are you hungry?" That's what she called Cortez. He said, "I'll eat later," and he went upstairs.

Kassie went into the kitchen and started cooking. She made the same thing that we would eat time and time again, rice and beans and whatever else she was going to cook. By this time, Gabrielle, Jonice, and I were watching television and just talking. While we were sitting there, Gabrielle checked her answering machine, and there was this one message: "Hey Gabrielle, this is Jeff. Give me a call when you get a chance." I just had this sinking feeling when I heard that message. Little did I know the person on that call would haunt my relationship with Gabrielle.

It was starting to get late, and everybody went upstairs to go to bed. I just laid there on the couch, thinking about the date and how fantastic it was and how comfortable I was being there with Gabrielle's family. Gabrielle always had this uncanny ability to make me feel like I was the only man in her life while I was with her, and I think that's what kept us together for a couple of years. It wasn't an extremely long time, but it was the longest amount of time I had ever been in a relationship that serious.

We ended up spending the next day together with her family at her sister's house. I got to meet much of the family, and they were all great. It was like Gabrielle and I had been married for years, and this was just another fun-filled day with the extended family. After several hours, Gabrielle asked if I was ready to go. We hugged and kissed everyone and said our goodbyes. When we got back to Gabrielle's house, Kassie said, "Gabrielle, I know you're not going to make Robert sleep on the couch again." It was awkward, but when Kassie and Jonice were gone, Gabrielle said, "You don't have to sleep on the couch. If you want to sleep in the bed, you can." And that was it. We ended up spending the night together. It just seemed so surreal because I'd never been in a situation where I felt that way about someone and then suddenly had what seemed to be a ready-made family.

The next day, I went back to New York and told Mark about the weekend that I'd had. The first question he asked was how she looked. I didn't have any pictures of her, but I described her to Mark. Mark knew me well. He said, "I doubt if it will last a month." Mark knew I typically didn't stay with one women for an extended period, but I told him Gabrielle was different.

I think I went down to Philly every weekend for the next few months. Sometimes I even went down there during the week. We spent a large amount of time together, but I started to notice that things were a little odd, and it turned out that Gabrielle was actually seeing someone else. I'm not sure how it came up. I don't know if Jeff called again, or whatever the case may be, but somehow, we got on the topic of relationships, and she told me that there was somebody else and that she cared a great deal for him. I was heartbroken, but not so much that I was ready to not be with her. We basically said that we would continue to see each other, but that it wouldn't be a "committed relationship." I agreed to it at the time, but over the next few months it was extremely difficult for me. As time went on, I realized that I had fallen in love with Gabrielle.

LIFE LESSONS

The summer was ending, and I had to go back to Atlanta to prepare for the upcoming recruitment season. By this time, I had seventeen schools that were CBCA Member Institutions. I had to try to focus on the company, but my head was reeling from what I had experienced with Gabrielle. When I was away from her, I was thinking about her constantly.

Ernie lived in a cul-de-sac with eight homes on a golf course. Once, I was having a conversation on the golf course with a friend from college named Christopher, who was in the music business. He was working with this popular R&B group at the time. When I told him what I was doing, he said excitedly, "Man, that's hot! Can we get the group involved? They could potentially become the spokespeople for the CBCA, and I know the record company would buy into it." We left the course, and Christopher said that he would call me the following week once he checked with the group and the record company. He called that next day and told me that the record company and the group loved the idea of being a spokesperson for the CBCA. I will never forget that phone call; I was jumping up and down in the bed thinking, "Wow, this is it. This is what I have been waiting for. Finally, I will not have to struggle anymore. No more sleeping on floors and in cheap hotels."

But Christopher called me back within minutes and said, "I have some bad news." I was still jumping on the bed when he said, "The record company changed their mind and decided not to do the deal." I was in total disbelief. To say that I was disappointed would greatly mischaracterize what I was feeling at that moment.

NEW MARKETING COLLATERAL

I went back to making photocopies of the applications. I would send some out to high schools and take some with me when I would go to the college fairs. One day, I was at Office Depot making copies, and when I went to pay for them, the person that was checking me out looked at what I was having printed and asked, "Is this a college application?" I said yes and began to tell him about the CBCA. "Wow, that's interesting." He told me that his name was Walter and went on to say, "I can make this application look a hell of a lot better. I'm a graphic artist, and if you're interested, I can show you what I can do with it." I said, "Absolutely." He told me he would put something together that night and to come back tomorrow to see what he had done. This was definitely one of those moments that God was showing me that I was on the right path and encouraging me to be persistent and not to give up. Walter coming into my life at that point in time was a turning point. I went home feeling a lot better about things. I couldn't wait until tomorrow.

I got up early the next day and went back to Office Depot, and he showed me the application he had created. My application had been the front and back of one sheet of paper. Walter had created a four-page application that you would fold. In my mind, this was the absolute best application I had ever seen. It was in color, professionally done, and I was blown away. "Walter, this is amazing. I cannot thank you enough. How much do I owe you?" I think he may have charged me twenty-five dollars, if that. At that time, even twenty-five dollars was a lot of money to pay. However, because Walter had done such a professional job, I had to make the sacrifice and pay him.

That was the start of the next phase of the CBCA. That application gave the service credibility, because I didn't have this crude piece of paper. I now had an application that was representative of the service, and in education, it's imperative to establish credibility. Because so few educational services were associated with a fee at that time, having this application helped to open a lot of doors when I wasn't there to explain about the company myself. I was sending this application to schools across the country, and it made the CBCA look like a viable educational service.

I was excited about going back on the road, and by this time I had started to collect the addresses of high school counselors and put together counselor packages with a letter of introduction and about ten applications to send to high schools nationwide. Things were really starting to take off with the CBCA. I was about to open up a bank account. I thought I was going to have problems doing it, because I had tried to open a personal bank account, and I was denied because of my credit. But a really good friend of mine, Nina, helped me to write the Articles of Incorporation, and we were able to get a Tax ID number. But as much as things were looking up as far as the company was concerned, my social life was in a shambles.

Although I wasn't in a committed relationship with Gabrielle at this point, I'd fallen deeply in love with her. I knew that she had this other person in her life. Every waking moment that I wasn't thinking about the CBCA, I was thinking about her potentially being with someone other than me. I wasn't able to enjoy the moment and the few successes that I was beginning to achieve. When I went back on the road again, this time I made it a point to go to Philadelphia first because I wanted to spend some time with Gabrielle. Then I would go to Chicago and then on to D.C. and Los Angeles.

By now, Gabrielle had moved to a townhouse in Blackwood. Something happened while I was there. We didn't get into an argument, necessarily, because that's not something that we did. But during the course of our talking, I think that may have been the first time she told me that she was actually in love with this other guy. To be lying there with someone that you love to the extent that I loved Gabrielle and to have her tell you that she's in love with someone else, I can't begin to tell you how I felt. I was just numb. I'm not sure how I managed to get through the next twenty-four hours. I called her a couple of times, and she didn't answer. I called again, and this time she answered and said, "Don't call me anymore."

I had to drive to Detroit that day to go to a college fair. I listened to Phyllis Hyman the whole way from Philadelphia to Detroit and cried the entire time. I ended up going back to Atlanta and just going through a range of emotions. Again, the CBCA was starting to pick up, but I was in love, and there was no controlling it. I could barely get out of bed. I was crying much of the day just trying to figure it out. I remember watching *Sleepless in Seattle*, and in the movie Tom Hanks talks about what it's like to try to get over being in love. He said, "You start each and every morning by reminding yourself to breathe until you don't have to remind yourself anymore." On that very day, at that very second, I began to heal.

I was still calling Gabrielle, and after about three or four days, she finally picked up. We talked, and she agreed to see me. Within hours, I was in my car on the way to Philadelphia. When I got there, I stayed in a hotel at the airport. Gabrielle was going to come see me after she got off from work. Waiting alone in that hotel, contemplating all of the things that could possibly happen made each and every second that much more agonizing. Finally, there was a knock at the door.

I opened the door and looking at Gabrielle, I was instantly reminded of the first day we met and how much I couldn't stand the thought of not having her in my life. I wasn't sure if I should hug her, kiss her, or just let her in and move away from the door. I did not want to jeopardize what little chance I might have to reconcile with her. I decided to just let her in and move away from the door. I asked if I could take her coat, and she said no, that she would not be staying long. I did everything I could to fight back the tears, thinking that this could possibly be the last time I would see her. She saw the disappointment on my face, and that's when she said something that allowed me to take a deep breath for the first time in months. She told me that while we were on the phone during our last conversation, the way that I'd expressed what I felt for her had made her see me in a different light. Unfortunately, without me realizing it at the time, the very moment that I knew Gabrielle was also in love with me, I started to pull away. It's something I had feared would happen because it's fairly characteristic of me.

CONTEMPLATING MATRIMONY

For the time being, though, things were going great. I had picked up a couple of sponsors for the CBCA. Gabrielle had actually gone with me to a meeting, and Gabrielle is a consummate professional. She walked into that meeting immaculately dressed, looking like a model who had just stepped off the runway. Having her there gave me confidence. Our first sponsorship was Educaid, a precursor to Wachovia. We came home excited. We celebrated with the kids by having a pizza party. Gabrielle and I were seriously talking about getting married.

I came back to Atlanta that fall. Although the CBCA was going fairly well, I was seriously thinking about giving it up at this point because it wasn't going well enough for me to be able to provide for Gabrielle and the kids. I went on Hire.com and applied for a sales position with K12 Learning Services (KLS). Some time went by, maybe a couple of weeks, and I got a phone call. The company was interested in scheduling an interview. It went well, and they hired me to be a sales rep. That was the moment that the CBCA was truly saved because I didn't know how I was going to survive. The salary KLS paid me helped me to sustain the CBCA. It also helped me to supplement my mother's income because she was beginning to need some financial help.

I was elated. It was more money than I'd ever made working in admissions. The base salary was sixty thousand dollars plus commission. That was far more than I had ever earned. KLS is a test prep service, and my primary job was to sell SAT and ACT test prep services to schools and school districts. My main territory was Georgia. It was an ideal position in that I was able to work from home. This allowed me to continue to run the CBCA while I was working for them.

KLS SAVES THE CBCA

Allen Davidson was the Director of Sales for my region and was the person who hired me. He is one of the brightest people that I've ever met. All of the people working at KLS were extremely bright. A lot of my insecurities about my intelligence resurfaced during that period. Developing a SAT/ACT test prep tool is a complicated process. There were countless times throughout my stint as a sales rep for KLS where I didn't feel like I had full grasp of what was going on, and that exacerbated my insecurities.

Allen went with me on my very first sales call to a high school somewhere in South Georgia. We offered three different types of test prep. There were print materials, an online tool, and KLS-taught classes. Clearly, I was not a good sales rep because I can't even remember all the different components. We were supposed to be making a presentation, and because I had only an elementary understanding of test prep and what went into the development of a test prep tool, to say my presentation was less than informative would be generous. It should have been obvious to Allen on that first sales call that I didn't necessarily have the skillset to do well. The only thing that helped me was my personality.

I think Allen felt, or at the very least he hoped, that I would eventually develop the skillset to become a successful. Allen and I rode together, and we didn't talk a lot on the way back from that first presentation. I'm sure he was wondering if he'd made the right decision about hiring me. I think I finally told him that I realized things hadn't gone well, and he reassured me by saying, "Don't worry about it. It's your first sales call. You'll get better."

A number of significant events happened within this time period. One was that I moved from living with Ernie to living in Camden Brookwood. This was in the summer of 2002. I had about $5,000 in the bank, and I was finally making enough money to move into my own place. I was also making money from the CBCA. I don't even remember how I found Camden Brookwood. I truly did not think that I was going to pass the credit check because of the time I'd been evicted. I assumed that would still be on my record. I filled out the application, paid the fee, and to my amazement, they approved me. I was elated.

I wanted to get back to Atlanta because Fayetteville was just so far from the city. The apartments had been built within the last two years. The grounds were gated and finely manicured. I moved into an apartment on the third floor, facing a wooded area. It was just everything I wanted. I just loved that apartment, and things were really looking up.

The only thing that was not going well was that this was about three or four months into the job, and I still hadn't sold any test prep services. KLS was considered a relatively small division then. When I first started working there, the largest deals in terms of dollar amount averaged around $7,500. Even though the sales goals weren't that high, I still hadn't really sold anything.

By now, the company had hired Winston Coles as Director of Sales. I remember looking at my numbers one night after a sales call, and they were dismal. By now, I had come to the conclusion that I was not going to be with the company for an extended period, but Winston was the consummate Sales Manager. He was an eternal optimist. When I told him I was down about my numbers, he said, "Robert, don't worry about it. Things will work out. You'll get it. Just keep pushing. Just keep working your funnel. You can do it." I understand that his bonus was contingent on my doing well, but I always felt like Winston cared about me as a person, and I learned that is a vital quality if you are going to successfully manage people.

I think I told Winston that night that in my heart of hearts, I was not a salesman. I had to believe in what I was doing so much that when I talked to people about it, it wasn't selling, it was sharing. For example, with the CBCA, when I walked into a school district, or a principal's office, or a superintendent's office, or into a state Department of Education, I was selling in a literal sense. However, because I believe so much in the CBCA and what it can do to help break the cycle of poverty in students' families, it didn't feel like sales. It felt like I was doing all that I could to try to increase the quality of life for students and their families.

I didn't bring that same passion and commitment to working for KLS. Obviously, if students increased their test score, that would increase their chances of getting into the institutions that they might be interested in attending or increase their chance of receiving a scholarship. But I didn't know enough about test prep to believe in it. It wasn't a part of my DNA. When I hung up after having that conversation with Winston that night, I knew that it was just a matter of time before I was fired. It was a sinking feeling because I had only been in my new apartment for few months, and I was making more money than I had ever made before. The thought of potentially losing my job with KLS and that source of income was disheartening.

OFFER TO BUY THE COMPANY

In November 2003, we had a sales meeting in Philadelphia. By now, one of the sales reps named Nicole had landed a contract with Philadelphia Public Schools that was going to be worth millions of dollars. Just a few months prior, the biggest deal that the K-12 division had ever secured was $7,500. Now they were in the throes of doing a million-dollar deal. During the sales meeting, The Philadelphia School Superintendent spoke to the salesforce, and after his presentation, Abram Rollins, the president of the K-12 division, came up to me and said, "Robert, can I speak to you for a second?" We went off to the side and sat down, and

Abram caught me off-guard when he said, "Allen has told me about this online application that you have where students can apply to several colleges. Tell me a little about the CBCA."

I had previously told Allen that my brother was running the CBCA. I hadn't really wanted to say anything about it or talk a lot about it because I didn't want them to think that I was still running the CBCA at the same time I was working for KLS. I was a little hesitant, but then I thought, what the hell? I didn't have anything to lose because I was probably on the verge of being fired anyway. So I told Abram, "Yes, I have this service. I've had it for a little over seven years. Students are able to use one application to apply to several different Historically Black Colleges and Universities."

We talked a bit more, and he asked me about the utilization of the application, how many schools participated in the program, and how many students had completed applications in the last few years. I told him we were averaging about four thousand students completing the application annually. Then he said, "What would you think if I were to make you an offer to buy the company?" I was completely out of my element at this point, because again, there I was, a kid from the Projects who went to Virginia State. I had an idea to create this common application and now Abram Rollins, representing KLS, was saying they were interested in buying my company.

I asked him what kind of offer he had in mind, and he said, "Well, what if we gave you $200,000?" Without hesitation, I said, "No. I would have to decline the offer." I didn't make a counteroffer, and he didn't ask me to. Fortunately, I had made enough working for KLS and the CBCA was doing well enough that I wasn't in a position where I felt like I had to sell the company. I found it fairly ironic that KLS was making me an offer to buy the company, and it was because of KLS that I didn't have to sell it.

I had no interest in selling the company; however, I said, "What if we establish a partnership? Because we both know I'm not going to make it as a salesperson. If you haven't already, I'm sure you and Winston are going to have to talk about letting me go. KLS is trying to make inroads in urban school districts throughout the country, and we can help with that because students are able to use the CBCA to apply to all these HBCUs, and our primary demographic is students of color."

One thing I will say about Abram and the KLS at the time, they were extremely socially conscious. Under Abram's leadership, the KLS division made a concerted effort to do all they could to mitigate the skill gaps of students of color as it related to test prep. We had had several conversations about it. Knowing that Abram was committed to helping students of color, I had no problem at all formulating this partnership.

He said, "Great. Why don't you come to New York? We'll sit down and hash out some type of agreement, and we'll move forward." Shortly after the meeting in Philadelphia, I flew to New York to meet with Abram. We established an agreement whereby KLS would pay me a $60,000 base fee and $10 for each application over a thousand.

The partnership with KLS helped to establish a sound financial foundation for the CBCA. I will always contend that if it had not been for KLS in general and Abram more specifically, the CBCA probably would not have survived. I was truly considering marrying Gabrielle, and I would have needed to have a stable source of income to take care of her and the kids.

By now, Gabrielle and I decided that we were going to start a monogamous relationship. All was good. Things were going well professionally; my social life was great. I had Gabrielle, and I started to think of Jonice and Cortez as my own children. I was practically spending every weekend in Philly. I hadn't actually bought a ring, but Gabrielle and I were definitely talking about getting married. As I said, though, from the moment we really became committed to each other, I had begun ever so slightly to pull back, and over the next few months after the meeting in Philly, I stopped seeing Gabrielle in the same light and started to pull back even more.

As an example, I was driving from Philadelphia to Indianapolis for the Circle City Classic. The Classic is an annual event that brings together two HBCUs to play one another in a football game. A major college fair is always held in conjunction with the Classic. While I was driving to Indianapolis, Gabrielle called me four or five times. It was the first time since we had met that I didn't rush to return her phone call, and I knew at that point that it was the beginning of the end of our relationship.

CBCA ONLINE APPLICATION

Mark Green had moved by this time and married Camille, and they had a house in Teaneck. Anytime I would go to New York to do school visits or participate in college fairs, I would always stay with Mark. This particular year when I was staying with Mark, I got an email from Jim Evans. I don't remember the company he was with, but the email said that they had been tracking the progress of the CBCA, and he thought he might be able to help me create an online application. He left his number. I called him almost immediately. That call was a godsend.

We hit it off right away. I told Jim how I'd gone from five schools to about twenty-four at that point, and he told me about how he and his partner would be interested in building an online application for me. It was definitely something I was very much interested in doing, so we started talking about cost. They wanted $15,000. I was doing fairly well at that point, but I remember saying no, I would be more inclined to pay them a base fee and then give them a percentage of each application fee. Jim talked to his partner, and they agreed. We agreed that I would pay them a base fee of $5000 and a five-dollar-per-application fee. Within a few weeks, Jim had built the online application.

I didn't spend much time talking to his partner. The few times that we talked, there was always some friction, but my friendship with Jim was growing with each conversation. They set up the database so that students could start to apply online using the CBCA. This created an opportunity for students to complete the application no matter where they were in the world. This was a watershed moment for the company.

When I got back home, I decided that it was time for me to rent some office space. Although I didn't have people that would be coming to the office, I needed a place for some data entry clerks and to have someone who could answer the phone. That was 2005. I rented an office space in Buckhead at Crowne Office Suites, across from the Lenox Mall in Atlanta. Paula, my accountant, introduced me to the owner of Crowne Office Suites.

After some negotiations about what I was willing and able to pay, the leasing agent showed me a room in the back of the building. The room didn't have any windows, and it was barely larger than a closet. It was just big enough to put two desks and two people in there. I paid maybe four hundred dollars a month. I felt a real sense of accomplishment when I got that office. I hadn't thought about how I was going to staff it yet, but just having an office seemed to me at the time to be a significant step forward for the company.

UNIQUE IN EVERY WAY

Those first few months or so, my nephew, Quent, had come down to go to school, and I thought that he might be able to work for me. However, due to classes he was taking for school, he was not able to dedicate as much time as I needed to have him in the office. Then I thought maybe my brother could do it, and that didn't work out either. I called Kevin Williams, who was the Director of Admissions at Clark Atlanta University, and asked if he knew anybody at CAU that I could depend on who was looking for work. This was going to have to be somebody who could work completely without supervision, because I was hardly ever going to be there. Kevin said, "As a matter of fact, I do. Her name is Unique Jones. She would be excellent."

He put me in touch with Unique. I talked to her, and she was impressive. I told her to stop by the office so we could talk. When Unique arrived, we talked for about an hour. She answered all of my questions, and she was very professional. Finally, Unique convinced me that she would be able to work independently.

I offered her the job. Unique was a model employee. She was one of the hardest workers I've ever known, and I never had any problems with her. She wouldn't see me more than once a month. Unique practically ran the company from the cramped office on Lenox Road.

Unique also helped me to learn some very valuable lessons. One day I was in the office with Unique, and I was talking to a student on the phone. When I ended the call, Unique felt as if I was being dismissive to the student. She stressed how important it was that I valued each and every student that completed the CBCA.

As time went on, we got so busy that the work was getting to be too much for Unique to do alone. She was having to manually enter the data for thousands of student applicants. Although we had an online application, we were still allowing students to complete a paper application. I asked Unique if she knew anyone who might be interested in working with us. We tried hiring one young lady, and she lasted about a week. I think Unique stayed with me up until maybe 2017, when we hired Lanice Alters, and Lanice stayed two years after Unique left.

Almost immediately after Lanice got there, I came into the office one day and Unique's demeanor had changed. We were starting to have more conversations about the amount of money that she was making and how often she would be paid. We didn't have any of those conversations until Lanice came, so I was assuming that Lanice was the origin of that. Though Unique and

I still had a great relationship, it was never quite the same once Lanice got there.

G.A.M.E. INITIATIVE WITH NBA TEAMS

We now had thirty-two schools on the Common Black College Application. We were starting to work with school districts throughout the country. My line brother at Virginia State, William Gordner, who worked for the Atlanta Hawks at the time, contacted me one day because he heard about our work in school districts and said that two hundred tickets had been donated. He asked if I wanted him to give the tickets to students that completed the CBCA. As we continued talking about it, we decided to do what would eventually become known as the Getting African American and Latino Males Educated (G.A.M.E.) Initiative. We partnered with local school districts to invite their students to participate in this G.A.M.E. event. The first event with the Hawks was a great success. It was held at the Hawks arena. As the students arrived, they were given G.A.M.E t-shirts, and we took group photos. We then held a general session in the Hawks arena.

We had several presenters, including a City Councilman, the announcer for the Atlanta Hawks, who was also a DJ on a local radio station, and Pat Daniels, my classmate from graduate school. The G.A.M.E. event went so well that the Atlanta Hawks entered the event on the NBA's Best Practices website, and we ended up getting phone calls from throughout the League inquiring about doing similar events with their teams. That next year, we did thirteen G.A.M.E. Events.

Lanice knew somebody that worked for Best Buy, and this individual had put me in touch with a regional person, and we ended up getting to Mike Doyle, who was a Regional Manager with Best Buy. We explained to him what we were doing, and he was on board right away. He immediately did all he could to get Best Buy Corporate on board. Ultimately, Mike arranged for me to meet with executives from Best Buy Corporate to talk about the

G.A.M.E. initiative and what we were looking to do with teams throughout the league.

As I prepared for the meeting with the Best Buy executives in Minneapolis, I took a minute to reflect on how far I had come—I was reared by a single parent in the Lincoln Terrace Projects, and in the next hour, I would be sitting in a meeting with some of the leading executives of Best Buy, talking to them about the G.A.M.E. event and how what we were doing throughout the country could potentially be used to augment their recruitment efforts for high school students. I owe a great deal to Mike Doyle.

In addition to arranging for me to meet with Best Buy Corporate, Mike put me in touch with their regional person in Denver, where we conducted one of the largest G.A.M.E. events of that year. We also visited a Best Buy store as a part of the outreach. Best Buy was a tremendous sponsor for three years, and much of that support can be directly attributed to Mike. To this day, Mike and I stay in constant contact on social media.

That same year, James Stotts, who was in HR at Clark Atlanta University, had a financial aid connection to Sallie Mae. Sallie Mae was a company that serviced college student loans. He put me in touch with Morris Gathers, and we talked about Sallie Mae coming on board as a National Sponsor for the G.A.M.E. events. Morris thought it was a great idea, and he arranged for me to meet with the Director of Marketing at Sallie Mae's corporate office. The meeting went extremely well, and they came on board. Both Best Buy and Sallie Mae were six-figure sponsors for three years, and we still had the KLS partnership.

We had more than 5,000 students over a three-year period participate in the game events, with teams that included the Atlanta Hawks, Charlotte Hornets, Memphis Grizzlies, Philadelphia 76ers, Denver Nuggets, Los Angeles Lakers, Orlando Magic, Washington Wizards, Houston Rockets, Minnesota Timberwolves, and the Miami Heat, and this is when Miami had just won the championship.

Around the time that we were doing the G.A.M.E. events, we also created a View Book. A View Book is promotional booklet full of pictures that colleges and universities use as a recruiting tool. Our View Book, which was like a mini magazine, included every school participating in the CBCA. Each of the thirty-two schools participating in the CBCA had their own ad. We modeled our View Book after a book that Ford and Ebony published for HBCUs. Our ultimate goal at the time, although we never achieved it, was to create an actual magazine.

A couple of things about the View Book were significant. The View Book allowed us to get larger sponsors. They didn't pay a lot of money, necessarily, but these were large companies: Coca Cola, Kraft, Delta Airlines, Westin Hotel, and Educaid (Wachovia). The View Book served as a valuable resource to help generate revenue for the G.A.M.E. events.

One of the events that helped the CBCA to garner some national recognition was my appearance on a nationally syndicated radio show. William arranged for me to do the interview along with Dr. Cheryl Mason, a counselor at the Detroit High School for the Fine and Performing Arts. Dr. Mason was a major supporter of the CBCA, and she practically mandated that her students complete the application.

The interview went extremely well. The host of the show asked me questions about how the company was started and the benefits of the CBCA to the HBCU Member Institutions. Dr. Mason explained how students were receiving millions in scholarship dollars and multiple acceptance letters by completing the CBCA.

We created a CD that contained this interview. We began to send out packets that included the View Book, the CD, and copies of the full-color application. The publicity from the appearance on that radio show really helped to lend credibility to the CBCA.

Most of our sponsors stayed with us for three or four years. What I learned from all of this was how powerful it is just to make phone calls. Out of the six or seven phone calls that I made soliciting sponsorships, rarely did a company tell me no. We obtained four sponsors, and obviously our ability to do that speaks to the viability of the service, the significance of what we were doing, and to the fact that we were beginning to gain recognition as a reputable educational service.

Around this time, I bought my first luxury car. I was able to put it in the company's name. The company was doing extremely well at this point. We had the KLS contract. We had some six-figure sponsorships from Best Buy and Sallie Mae. We also had the sponsorships from Coca Cola, Delta Airlines, Kraft Foods, and Educaid Wachovia, the precursor to Wachovia, which ultimately became Wells Fargo. I had moved from one side of the apartment complex where I lived to the other. I now lived on a top floor with a loft feel and a lot more space. It really felt like I had accomplished something.

Because we were doing so well in terms of the revenue streams from the sponsorships and the KLS partnership, I didn't pay that much attention to the amount of revenue that we were generating via the application, nor did I pay any real attention to the amount of revenue that we were generating via the licensing fees that the member institutions paid to be a part of the service. For the first time, my life had some semblance of normalcy.

One day, I was in D.C. to do a presentation at Archbishop Carroll High School. Will was also in D.C., working with a female professional basketball player. He was trying to arrange some public speaking engagements for her. Will asked if she could come with me to present to the Archbishop Carroll students. I agreed to let her say a few words during the course of my presentation. Will and the basketball player met me at the high school.

I arrived at the school early and went down to speak to the counselor, Sister McColloch. While I was in Sister McColloch's office, one of the students walked in and asked me, "Is William Gordner with you?" I said yes. Somehow Will had managed to talk his way into having the ball player speak to the class before my presentation started. I was livid because I had told Will I didn't want that to happen. I didn't want the school to think that a ball player was affiliated with me in any way. Will and I got into a big argument outside of the school. I remember telling Will I loved him to death but there was no way in hell that I was going to allow what he was trying to do to jeopardize my business. I was attempting to encourage the Archbishop Carroll students to complete the CBCA. I didn't have a clue what this ballplayer was saying to the students. She could have said the wrong thing to those students, and I could have been barred from the school.

From that day forward, the relationship between Will and I was never the same. I haven't spoken to him in about two years. We had gone through so much together, and the thought of not having him as a close friend was disheartening.

Within days of Will and I having that argument, and while I was still trying to process what had happened, I was informed by Unique that Abram Rollins had left KLS. Abram and I had established a valued friendship over the course of the partnership between KLS and the CBCA, but KLS was not as committed to the partnership once Abram left.

That very next year, when the contract ended and we were negotiating the next contract, KLS only wanted to pay half of what they had been paying. But more important, it was clear during the negotiations that their focus had changed. That was extremely disconcerting to me because that KLS contract was a significant revenue source for us. I felt like my quality of life and the success I had achieved with the business would be jeopardized if we lost the KLS contract.

The revenue from the applications was becoming a significant revenue stream, and we had also increased the number of colleges participating in the service. We had thirty-seven HBCUs at this point, and more of the schools were starting to pay a membership fee to be a part of the CBCA. These revenue streams made up for the money that we lost from the KLS contract being scaled back, but that next year KLS ended the partnership totally. With Abram gone, there was no one left there that cared enough about continuing the contract with the CBCA.

LAUSD: BUNNY WITHERS

I was asked to present at a Los Angeles Unified School District School Counselor Conference on the University of Southern California campus. After the presentation, a woman named Bunny Withers approached me. She was wearing a very colorful dress with matching earrings and purse. I really admired her sense of fashion. Bunny attended Texas Southern University. We started talking, and she was very much interested in the CBCA, how it worked, and how students completed the application. We ended up going to lunch to continue talking about the CBCA. At that time, the Los Angeles Unified School District was divided up into thirteen smaller districts. Bunny was over some special programs in District Seven. She started to think about how she could use some of her funding to pay for students in District Seven, which had four high schools at the time, to complete the CBCA. We had several district-wide contracts in other states that were underwriting the cost for students to complete the CBCA.

Bunny asked me to submit a proposal, and she said that her superintendent was extremely interested. We talked about the district paying a flat fee for all the students throughout the four high schools to use the CBCA. By this time we had lost the G.A.M.E. contracts with Best Buy and Sallie Mae, and we were winding down in terms of the number of events that we were doing with the different NBA teams, so this new contract was very timely and was a primary source of revenue. We agreed that the district would pay $35,000 for all high school seniors to complete the CBCA at no cost. As a part of that contract, we would visit the four high schools and facilitate the completion of the application.

The initial contract lasted five years. We then started to realize that it was important to reach back and to have middle school students begin to think about attending college. Bunny and I talked about the goal of creating a college matriculation culture, so we decided to do an initiative for Black and Hispanic male middle school students. It was one of the most rewarding things that I have ever done. We called it the "Minority Middle School Male Initiative."

We held a workshop every week for nine weeks in each of the five middle schools in the district. Each school had twenty students participate. In addition to focusing on the importance of education, we did workshops on topics including conflict resolution, test-taking techniques, and personal grooming. I learned so much about life, talking to these young brothers about some of the challenges that they faced. Some of these students had to walk across several gang territories just to get to school and back. Hearing those kinds of stories was heartbreaking.

We decided to do a couple of things that we felt would have an impact on the students in the program. First, we took them to a local college fair. The goal was to give them the opportunity to meet with representatives from different HBCUs. Second, at the end of the nine weeks, we held a graduation ceremony for the students at McCormick & Schmick's on Rodeo Drive. We were running late to get there, and I was asking if we could take the Interstate because it would be quicker from South Central. One of the principals pulled me aside and said, "Rob, we'd much rather take surface streets because many of these students have never been beyond their neighborhood. This is going to be their first real opportunity for them to see something beyond the three or four blocks that they're basically relegated to." So of course, that's what we did. When we got to McCormick & Schmick's, and as the students got off the bus, they began to see stores like Gucci, Prada, and Louis Vuitton.

The look on their faces was priceless. After having dinner, we ended with an awards ceremony. We called each student individually to the front and gave them a certificate. It was one of the most heartwarming and emotional experiences I've ever had, just seeing those students smiling from ear to ear as they accepted their certificates. I often wonder what happened to those students that participated in the Minority Middle School Male Initiative and how many of them made it out of South Central. I thank God for bringing Bunny into to my life. She has been a trusted colleague and friend since the very day we met. Her commitment to education and students of color is unsurpassed.

By this point, the G.A.M.E. events had stopped. This was around the time of the housing bubble market crash. The sponsorships that we had with Sallie Mae and Best Buy also ended. Now I really didn't know where to turn. We went from making around $350,000 a year to around $200,000 a year at best, and that was a significant loss of revenue for a small company. I still had Unique and Lanice on the payroll. Fortunately, at this time, my mom was still working, so I wasn't taking care of all of her finances at this time, I was only supplementing her income, but I knew the time would come when she would be primarily financially dependent on me.

Those were some lean years up until around 2016. I was relying more on application fees and the money that we were generating via contracts with the Member Institutions. Some friction was also beginning between Jim and me. Jim was the person who had created the CBCA online platform, and we were in desperate need of enhancing the functionality of the platform. The schools were beginning to complain about not being able to automatically enter our data into their database. They were still having to print the applications and manually enter the information that the students had provided into their systems. During this time, we did create a process by which students could upload their transcripts. This new process helped significantly because before that, Lanice,

Unique, or I were having to manually enter transcripts and test scores into the system, and we were processing thousands of applications. It was a difficult period for the company and me. Then one morning, I got a call from my brother. I could tell based on his tone that something was seriously wrong. All he said was, "Mom just had a stroke."

Nine

Mom is Sick

MOM HAD A STROKE: COME HOME

Nikki, one of my nieces, had gone to my mom's house and found her lying on the floor with a severe bruise on her head. She either hadn't taken her medicine, or she had taken the wrong medicine. We were never able to determine exactly what happened to her.

I immediately told my brother that I was on the way. I didn't think about it. I just threw some things in a bag and jumped in the car. My head was reeling at this point. I didn't know what was going to happen to my mom. At this time, she lived by herself. My brother Todd lived in Atlanta. Driving home, I felt a range of emotions. It was a seven-hour drive, and I cried intermittently the entire way home trying to keep from contemplating the worst. This was the first real emergency that we had ever had with my mom, and I was truly scared.

When I got home, I went straight to the hospital. The doctors weren't sure how much the stroke was going to affect her. The most the doctors knew was that at the moment, she was not able to speak normally. I was just reeling at this point. Over the next few days, Mom started to get better, and the doctors finally told us that she had just had a minor stroke. It affected her speech, but not her movement. It turned out that we just had to do these exercises with her to help both improve her speech and her ability to process information. He told us that she may have suffered some memory loss that she may not regain, but all in all, we were blessed that mom came away from the stroke without any more serious complications. She stayed in the hospital for a few weeks and then spent thirty days in a rehab facility. She had fully recovered except for some minor memory loss, but my whole world had turned upside down.

Although I was agonizing over the thought of having to move back to Roanoke, I was extremely doubtful that Mom was now going to be able to stay in Roanoke by herself. She had to retire from work. Mom had always been active. She walked. She got her nails and her hair done every Friday. She went to church. She was always doing something around the house. Todd came home for about a week or so, and we never really talked about what we were going to do moving forward. I knew that financially, I was not in a position to have someone live with Mom.

Two months after Mom's stroke, I was still in Roanoke and unsure of what to do next. I dreaded the thought of having to move back home; however, I was going to do what was best for Mom, even if I had to stay in Roanoke indefinitely. That was a tough time. Again, I was having problems with Jim, trying to get different things done to move the company forward, and to make matters worse, we weren't making a lot of money. I was really starting to feel the pressure of work because it was becoming more of a challenge to convince Jim to update the platform, and we were spending more time arguing about the direction of the company.

My not having a social outlet was exacerbating the problem, just making it more difficult for me to deal with everything every day. There was a comedy show at the Roanoke Civic Center, and I decided to go. While standing in line at the box office to buy my ticket, I was talking on my cell phone to a sponsor in Los Angeles. After I ended the call, I heard a female voice from behind me politely ask, "What's going on in LA?" I turned around and jokingly said, "Mind your business." We laughed, and it was the first time I had laughed or smiled in weeks. The inquisitive one introduced herself as Kianna Price. From that day forward,

Kianna and I have been the best of friends. She was there for me
during some very difficult times while I was in Roanoke, and I
am eternally grateful to her.

The Super Bowl was approaching. It was going to be played
in New Orleans. I desperately needed a break; I had to get away.
Mom was doing much better by now. She was talking, although
she still had some memory loss. My cousins promised to look in
on Mom while I was away, so I decided to drive to New Orleans.

Almost immediately after I got just outside of the Virginia
state line, I felt as if the weight of the world had been lifted from
my shoulders. In New Orleans, as I was checking into my hotel,
I ran into a fraternity brother named Jacob. He was a host on a
nationally televised entertainment show. Jacob invited me to the
San Francisco 49ers party after the game. Although the 49ers lost,
it was a great party. A superstar hip-hop artist performed. Up
until then, I had never been to a rap concert, and I was right in
front of the stage. It was a great show.

Immediately after the show, Jacob said, "Come on, we're going
backstage to the dressing room." The trip had already exceeded
my expectations after having been front row center stage at the
concert, but now we were going to the dressing room. Jacob said
something to the security guard who was standing in front of
some steps. I couldn't hear what he said because the music was
too loud. The security guard let us pass, and we walked up the
steps into a fairly large room that had a buffet table, a bar, and
several couches and chairs. The artist was sitting in one of the
chairs, surrounded by several people talking and laughing. Jacob
walked over to the artist, and as soon as the artist saw him, he
sprang to his feet and greeted Jacob as if they were old friends.
After a few minutes, Jacob waved for me to follow him and the
artist to a back room, where we went and sat down. The next
thing I knew, the artist lit a joint and passed it around to some
of the other guys that had joined us. Then he fired up another
joint and put it in rotation. Each time the brother sitting next

to me took a couple of tokes and looked at me and said, "You want to hit this?" I'd say, "Nah, I'm good," and they'd just pass it to somebody else. We were there no more than ten or fifteen minutes, and I'm almost sure that there were five to six joints being passed around within that time.

I was glad when Jacob finally suggested that we leave that room. I was starting to get high, and I hadn't smoked one joint. We spent the rest of the time enjoying the party until I decided to leave because I had a long drive back to Roanoke the next morning. I thanked Jacob and walked back to my hotel.

During the drive home, I came to the conclusion that if I was going to have to stay Roanoke, I needed to be prepared to make the best of the situation. Fortunately, Mom fully recovered except for some short-term memory loss. She started driving again and doing many of the things that she had done before her stroke. However, we had encouraged her to retire, and she was trying to get used to that. Things were going well enough that I was starting to feel more comfortable spending time away from Roanoke.

I was torn. I knew that I could not move home permanently. I also knew that I couldn't leave Mom there by herself. In the end, I decided to go back to Atlanta. That's when I got into the habit of calling or texting my mom every night, and I still do to this day. Since then, my brother Todd has moved home. He's been there with her now for about a year and a half. I respect Todd so much for making the sacrifice to come home and take care of my mom. I know it isn't easy for him. His selflessness was instrumental in helping me to feel comfortable knowing that Mom is taken care of, and it created the opportunity for me to focus on growing the CBCA.

CHANGES AT THE CBCA

Jim and I were starting to have heated discussions every other day about his inability to upgrade the platform. This was becoming increasingly frustrating because Jim was a single point of failure for me. If something were to happen to him, I would be lost. I didn't have any passwords, access codes, nothing. It may have been Jim's way of protecting his interest in the company. Regardless, it put me in a very vulnerable position.

To make matters worse, Unique, who had been my sole source of stability in the office, decided that she had to leave. That was tough because Unique's presence in the office had basically allowed me to go out and not even be concerned about what was going on in the office when I was away. Lanice was a good worker, but she just wasn't as dedicated as Unique.

By the time Unique left, we had stopped using a paper application entirely. Although Lanice wasn't having to manually complete the online applications anymore, she did have to manually enter transcript information, which was an extremely laborious process. It created a huge logistical problem for us with regards to providing transcripts to the various colleges. It was also the source of the problem I was having with Jim. I was asking him to do things that would automate and simplify the process for transferring data between us and our Member Institutions.

During this same time period, we were approached by a Fortune 500 company to partner with them in the creation of a CBCA mobile app. We decided to schedule a meeting with them at their corporate office in Los Angeles. Six people from different divisions of the company attended the meeting. Christian Samuel and I represented the CBCA. Without going into any great detail, let's just say the meeting didn't go well. We just didn't see eye-to-eye with two of the representatives from the company. They took the position that since the company was a nationally recognized brand, our contribution to the project would be minimal. Consequently, I should not expect to get the amount of money I was proposing that the CBCA receive.

This is when I stood up to leave. While looking directly at the two people that had expressed the objections, I said, "Clearly, we have reached a point of impasse, and there is not much need in continuing with the meeting."

As we were leaving the building, Christian told me that when he had stepped out of the meeting to get a drink of water, he could hear me raising my voice from the water fountain. At that moment, he knew the deal was not going to happen.

I was truly disappointed that we couldn't reach an agreement. This was one of several times I've contemplated over the years that if we could have established that partnership, the CBCA would have grown much faster. After that conversation with the Fortune 500 company, and thinking about my frustration with Jim, I began to look for other ways to grow the company.

Ten

A New Beginning

I decided to go to one of the nearby college campuses to find someone to help me create this app. I went to the Computer Science and Technology Building and asked around, "Who was the best student in terms of creating an app and coding?" The same name kept coming up: Kevin Roberts.

One of the students that knew Kevin gave me his number, and I called him. Within minutes, we were talking as if we had known each other for years. I told him what I wanted to do, and Kevin was exactly what I was looking for. He was knowledgeable, he was confident, and not once during the course of our conversation did he ask about money. That was important only because it gave me the impression that he was primarily concerned about the project and what I was attempting to do to help students of color. I have sometimes wondered how it is that I was able to meet two people who were ideal for me personally and professionally, because I am not that easy to work with. I definitely have an alpha-type personality, and I tend to think I have all the answers, but both Kevin and Jim were able to push beyond all of that and work together. I told Kevin what I wanted, and he said okay. He gave me some numbers in terms of how much it would cost to create this mobile app, and he built it.

My frustration with Jim was growing because it had gotten to the point where we needed to move to another server. We got into an argument because I was so frustrated with him not being able to do what needed to be done to move to this new platform.

He needed to fill out the necessary forms for a security certificate, and we couldn't do that because the computer language that Jim used to create the CBCA was antiquated, and it wasn't compatible with the security certificate specifications. He had worked for me for about fifteen years. I had been able to take care of my family and employees for many of those years as a result of what Jim had built, but Jim's system had outlived its usefulness. I eventually told Kevin I wanted him to start to work on a new platform because we had reached the point that we could no longer use the original system that Jim built.

I told Jim that we were going to have to take immediate steps to upgrade the CBCA platform. We had reached a point where the business relationship was no longer tenable. I felt bad about it because I owed Jim so much. If it weren't for him, there would be no CBCA, and I promised him that if ever sold the company, he would receive a percentage of the money. I think of Jim as a brother. He's like family to me. But I told him that we had to move away from his system and that we were going to start to use the new platform that Kevin had built. We agreed that Jim would continue to get a percentage of the application fees for that year and that he would get a lesser amount in the following year or two.

I'm sure Jim was disappointed, but I know he felt as I did, that he had taken the CBCA has far as he could. Almost right away, Kevin asked me what were the biggest challenges that we were having. I told him that the CBCA was functioning as it should, but we desperately needed to have a process that would allow students or counselors to upload their student's transcripts and for students to upload their test scores directly into the application, and Kevin created that capability.

As a result of Kevin's work, there was no longer any need to enter any documents manually. We had finally moved to a totally automated process, so I had no more need for any support staff at that point. I made the difficult decision to let Lanice go, and I shut down the office. That was a savings of about $50,000 a year. At the same time, Unique said that she would work from home part-time just to clean up whatever needed to be done.

We had created three different dashboards: one for high school counselors to upload student transcripts and view information; one for students that allowed them to view their completed application, see what schools had accessed it, and message those schools; and one for Member Institution Counselors to access information that had been submitted to them. The colleges had agreed to accept student transcripts through this system because counselors were creating accounts and uploading them. We scheduled training sessions with different Member Institutions, and they were excited about the new platform. We didn't deviate tremendously from what Jim had created because we had started to use counselor accounts, and the counselors were somewhat used to the system. Kevin had simply created some additional functionality as far as what the high school counselors were able to do.

Starting in September 2018, students were able to start to use the new application. The new CBCA platform was housed on the same url, so that we could take advantage of all of the traffic we had already established. That was a tremendous year for us. We were now totally paperless. This meant that we were able to run a fairly lean operation. We had had some regional reps that worked with us, but now there was no real need for them.

By this time, we were working with around sixty Member Institutions, and our first year on the new platform, we had close to 20,000 students complete the CBCA. This was nearly double what we had been doing before. One of the things that I'm certain helped to increase the number so significantly was that when a student went through the application process, it triggered an email being sent to their school counselor requesting them to upload the student's transcript. As you can imagine, when you're having 20,000 students completing the CBCA, that's a significant number of counselors that have to upload their student's transcript, a process which has the added benefit for us of them becoming familiar with the CBCA. They're seeing what we do, getting information about the Common Black College Application, and realizing how much their students can benefit from this streamlined process for applying to so many different HBCUs at one time. They tell other students about it, and things snowball from there.

Students that complete the CBCA are now in a position to receive acceptance letters, financial aid packages, and scholarship offers from several different HBCUs. Students that have done well in school have completed the CBCA and received millions in scholarship dollars and multiple acceptance letters. But equally as important, we want to create an opportunity for those students like myself, whose grade point average and test scores are not indicative of their college aptitude to attend college.

Now high school counselors nationwide, if not throughout the world, were starting to hear about the CBCA because students who had completed the application are being featured in national media outlets, including BET, *Ebony*, *USA Today*, *People*, *The New York Times*, and on several local and national television news outlets. At this point, we had established partnerships with some of the largest school districts in the country and with several college access programs. In 2018, we also received our first two large contracts. One contract was with the D.C. Office of State Superintendent of Education. The agreement allowed all students in D.C. public and charter schools to complete the CBCA for free. The second contract was with the Minneapolis Public Schools.

In late Fall 2018, while I was in a high school for a visit, I happened to see a competitor's poster, and it dwarfed everyone else's poster. Most of the other posters, including ours, were only 11" x 17", but in that moment, I realized that the competitor's poster had to be 2' x 3'. While I was standing in the school looking at the competitor's poster, I called my printer and told him to stop printing those 11" by 17" posters now. I wanted the print size changed to 2' x 3'. He said, "It's going to be expensive to change the poster size in the middle of a print job." I replied, "I don't care." We sent out close to 10,000 of the 2' x 3' posters that year. We jokingly referred to the posters as billboards because they were so large. I received so many calls from friends saying, "I was just in a high school, and I saw your poster." I mean, you could see it from all the way down in the hall. We've sent posters that size to high schools and community colleges every year since 2018, and we continue to send them.

Those three things—the updates to the platform, the school counselor transcript upload, and sending out the posters to thousands high schools nationwide—contributed to the CBCA becoming one of the most recognized educational services throughout the United States, Africa, and the Caribbean.

We are now in a place where a significant number of our CBCA Member Institutions have an automated process to transfer student data from our platform to their database. My plans for the future are to focus more on developing relationships and partnerships with schools, school districts, organizations, states, and countries.

THE PRODIGAL SON

I had been talking to Dr. Glover and Ora Douglas about trying to establish a national partnership. Dr. Glover is the International President of the Alpha Kappa Alpha Sorority, Inc. (AKA). She is also the President of Tennessee State University. Ora Douglas is the Alpha Kappa Alpha Sorority, Inc. leader of International Service Programs. Ora invited me to speak at the AKA Southern Leadership Conference about how the CBCA could be used with their #CAP Initiative.

The presentation went extremely well. I met members of the organization from all over the world, many of whom started to utilize the service. It was at that conference that I met

Anita Coleman, the Director of Special Events at Virginia State University. She posted on Facebook saying, "Robert, we need to get you as a speaker." Then she messaged me again and asked if I would send her my number so she could call me. I did so, and she called me a few minutes later and asked, "Would you consider being the Spring Convocation Speaker at Virginia State University?"

If I gave myself too much time to think about it, I knew I would said no. As I have said, I have always been apprehensive about speaking in public. I have become much more comfortable with it over the years, but I didn't have the confidence to speak to larger audiences like graduations, convocations, and banquets. I had always turned these types of invitations down. But I knew that in order to move the CBCA to the next level, I was going to have to do more in terms of public speaking engagements. So I immediately responded, "Yes I will speak at the Convocation." Anita said, "Rob, that's fantastic! I'll be in contact in the next few weeks."

This was probably around early August, and the speech was in September. Ordinarily, I would have started to get extremely nervous as soon as I hung up the phone, and started to doubt myself, but none of that happened. I've always had my angels, and I am a firm believer that God has put me here to do exactly what I am doing. I felt like this was Him saying to me, "It's time." I immediately started to think about the speech and the topics I wanted to address. That said, there were definitely times that month that I thought to myself, "What makes me think I have the oratorical skills to be a convocation speaker?" But then I thought about how so much of what happened to me that was consequential in my life happened while I was at Virginia State. My humanity was awakened on that campus. I was amazed to think that I was now being given an opportunity to stand on a stage at the institution that I love so dearly, and where I learned so much.

As I was starting to write the speech, I first looked at what other speakers had done. Then I realized that I didn't want this speech to be overly clinical or cerebral. I wanted it to come from my heart because I've found that when I have a tendency to get nervous speaking, it's usually because I'm not speaking from the heart. I started to think about various subjects, and I came up with three basic themes. One was the deleterious effect that social media is having on our society. The second was how debilitating self-doubt can be. This was particularly important to me because I had to learn how to manage self-doubt before I could begin to accomplish anything, and I knew that there are countless others grappling with the same problem. The third thing was the difference between being successful and being great. I wanted to make the point that we all define success in whatever way we see fit. For me, success is the ability to provide for oneself and one's family, but to be great is to be able to effect change in the lives of others.

As the date of the speech drew closer, I practiced several times a day. I didn't want to let a lot of people hear it before the actual speech, but I did let Mark hear it because I knew he would give me some honest feedback without being overly critical. I recited only the opening of the speech to Mark and told him the three topics I was going to address. With his voice full of excitement, he said, "Yo, that's a great opening, but you ought to talk about coming from the bottom to the top like Drake raps about in his song," because that's basically what I had done, but I knew I wasn't going to do that. Remember, Mark's background is in music, and I understood the reference, but I opted not to use the quote.

I was vacillating in terms of what I was going to do as far as inviting my family. Bear in mind, my mom is eighty-three, and she doesn't travel much. I just told her in passing that I was going to be giving a speech at Virginia State. I didn't specifically ask her to come until I was sure that my brother would be able to bring her. Then I called my Uncle Vick and asked if he and my aunt would like to be my guests at the speech, and he said without hesitation, "We will be there."

Somebody that knew me from Virginia State posted on social media that week, "Is Rob going to be wearing any socks?" because as I said, as an undergrad, I was known for not wearing socks. I had posted a picture of myself with no socks on Facebook a few days before the speech in jest and said, "What do you think?"

As it turned out, my brother was able to get off from work and bring my mom. We all met at the hotel, including Eric, my uncle Vick, and his family. Normally, when I have a speech or presentation, I start to get a little nervous as the time approaches for me to speak. But this was different. I just felt so at peace. We drove to campus and walked into the auditorium. I kept thinking that at some point I was going to start to get nervous, but I never did. Ron Neal walked in, and I introduced him to my family. Long ago, I had mentioned to Ron that my mom loves elephants, and he had remembered and brought my mom an elephant figurine. I told my mother that Ron was like family to me, and she gave him a big hug and thanked him for the elephant.

There was a reception beforehand, and they sat us at a table. We met various officials from Virginia State, and then President Abdulla came in and introduced himself to my family. Anita came over and told me it was time to take the stage. My family was shown to their seats. Dr. Duron asked if we were ready and then proceeded to usher Dr. Abdula and myself to the stage. We came out from behind the curtain and took our seats. As I looked out into the crowd, it felt like time had slowed down, and I felt such an extreme sense of calm.

First, the choir sang. There were a couple of speeches, and then the president stepped to the podium and began to introduce me. By now, I was starting to focus on the task at hand, and then I heard the president say, "I would like to introduce Robert

Mason, president and founder of the Common Black College Application."

I stood up and moved towards the podium. As I started to speak, I was overcome by a range of emotions because I was thinking about how many of the people that I love were there in the front row of the auditorium and how important this moment was to me. Something came over me as I started to speak. I've never thought of myself as an orator, but I could hear my voice rise and fall with a rhythmic cadence, pausing just enough for emphasis.

As far as I understand it from talking to people afterwards, the speech was well-received. My uncle said that the thing that impressed him the most was that I never looked down at my notes. It wasn't because I had necessarily memorized the speech,

Delivering the Convocation Speech at Virginia State University in 2019.

it was because I hadn't needed my notes. I had simply stood there at the podium and talked about my life.

Normally after a speech, I feel a sense of relief, but what I was feeling at that moment was far from normal. I felt such a sense of accomplishment, not just about that day, but about my life. Standing on that stage, I reflected on all that I had experienced over the past twenty years and how it had changed me. I had discovered my humanity. I had learned to cast aside my doubts and fears when faced with what might appear to be insurmountable odds and to keep going anyway. I had become unwilling to subscribe to conventional definitions of success and had dared, instead, to be great. As the crowd came to their feet and began to applaud, I thought about what my grandmother Mammaw used to say when I would come home: the Prodigal Son is home. As I stood there with tears in my eyes, I could hear all my angels in heaven and here on earth—my grandmothers Mammaw and She She, my dad and my mom, my aunts Gayle and Minnie, my uncles Will and Vic, my cousins Pierre and Sherry—all saying, "We love you, Rob." I whispered to Mammaw as if she was standing next to me, "Yes, Mammaw, the Prodigal Son is home."

Made in the USA
Middletown, DE
16 June 2023

32713839R00089